**THE LIBRARY**
MANAGEMENT, MOTIVATION
& DISCIPLINE

# INTERVENTIONS

Collaborative Planning for Students At Risk

## Procedural Manual

*A Resource for
Administrators, School Psychologists,
School Counselors, Classroom Teachers, Resource Teachers,
Behavioral Specialists, Mentor Teachers, and
Intervention Teams (SSTs, TATs, etc.)*

Randall Sprick • Marilyn Sprick • Mickey Garrison

Copyright © 1993 by
Randall Sprick, Marilyn Sprick, and Mickey Garrison
All rights reserved.

Edited by Jami Leutheuser
Text layout and design by Susan Krische
Cover design by Londerville Design

ISBN# 0-944584-95-0

Published and Distributed by:

**Sopris West**
1140 Boston Avenue • Longmont, Colorado 80501 • (303) 651-2829

# Acknowledgments

We would like to acknowledge the many teachers, administrators, psychologists, counselors, and others who have participated in the *Interventions* process. These highly skilled and caring individuals have provided valued guidance on how to make this material both practical and effective.

We would like to thank Lisa Howard, Jan Hasbrouck, and Jami Leutheuser for their thoughtful contributions as they helped edit and organize *Interventions*. We would also like to express our appreciation to Stu Horsfall and Duane Webb at Sopris West for their patience and collaboration through the development of this program.

We owe a special debt of gratitude to Betsy Norton with North Central Educational Services District. Betsy has made suggestions through the years that have helped shape the direction and content of our work.

Finally, we would like to thank our own children, Matt Sprick, Jessica Sprick, and Ty Garrison who teach us so much about life, learning, and joy.

# About the Authors

**Randall Sprick, Ph.D.** is an educational consultant and teacher trainer in Eugene, Oregon. Each year, Dr. Sprick conducts workshops and classes for over 5,000 teachers and administrators throughout the United States and Canada. Much of his work involves helping teachers set up classrooms that encourage student responsibility and motivation, while humanely and effectively helping problem students learn to behave in more responsible ways.

Dr. Sprick has developed numerous articles, books, audio tapes, and videotapes that assist school personnel in dealing with the issues of discipline and classroom management. Dr. Sprick has worked as an assistant professor at the University of Oregon and is an adjunct faculty member of the University of Oregon and Seattle Pacific University. He is a past president of the Association for Direct Instruction.

**Marilyn Sprick, M.S.** has worked as a regular classroom teacher, Chapter I Learning Specialist, and Special Education Resource Room Teacher in elementary and middle schools. Over the past decade, she has worked as an educational consultant and teacher trainer, assisting teachers with strategies for helping low-performing students manage the academic demands of the regular classroom.

Ms. Spricks' background and continued work with school districts, teachers, and students provides her with the ability to share practical, as well as effective strategies for adapting curricula and motivating students. Ms. Sprick teaches continuation courses for the University of Oregon and Seattle Pacific University.

**Mickey Garrison, Ph.D.** has had a wide variety of professional experiences during the past 20 years. She has taught in, and consulted with elementary and secondary general education programs, and in programs for students with emotional and behavioral disorders. She has assisted with the development and coordination of the University of Oregon's Classroom Consultation Training Program and the Parent Consultation Training Program.

Dr. Garrison provides training on school-wide discipline, proactive classroom strategies, effective behavioral interventions, and consultation.

# Overview of *The Library—Management, Motivation & Discipline*

*The Library—Management, Motivation & Discipline* is a set of practical materials designed to assist in creating productive, safe, and respectful learning environments. The materials are full of specific "how-to" information. Though each resource stands alone, all are designed around five basic concepts:

- All students must be treated with dignity and respect.
- Students can and should be taught skills for success.
- Motivation and responsibility should be encouraged through positive interactions.
- Misbehavior provides a teaching opportunity.
- Collaboration is critical—staff must work together to meet student needs.

## Components of the Library

*Interventions: Collaborative Planning for Students At-Risk* is both a resource and a process for education professionals. Through consultation and collaboration, staff members learn to share their expertise in developing practical intervention plans. Booklets describe how to set up, implement, and fade 16 major interventions. Interventions include procedures such as *Managing Physically Dangerous Behavior, Managing Severely Disruptive Behavior, Self-Monitoring, Self-Control Training, Restructuring Self-Talk,* and *Academic Assistance*. An optional 20 cassette audio tape album is available to accompany this program.

*Foundations: Establishing Positive Discipline Policies* assists staff in designing policies that create a calm, safe, and positive school climate. This site-based management approach to discipline allows staff to increase consistency, clarify expectations, improve positive interactions, increase student motivation, and reduce office referrals. Video and print materials provide step-by-step information on how to write, implement, and maintain a policy that actually guides daily practice.

Although still in the planning stages, subsequent resources in *The Library* include:

- *Substitutes: Planning for When the Teacher is Gone*
- *The Teacher's Encyclopedia of Discipline: 100 Problems/500 Plans*
- *The Teacher's Encyclopedia of Motivation: Preventing Problems/Creating Enthusiasm*
- *The Building Administrator's Guide to Discipline and Motivation*
- *Support Staff's Guide to Motivation and Discipline* (volumes include: *The Paraprofessional, The Bus Driver, The Music Teacher, The Physical Education Teacher,* and *The Librarian/Media Specialist*)
- *Family Involvement in Motivation and Discipline*
- *The Special Educator's Role in Motivation and Discipline*

# Table of Contents

How to Use *Interventions* .................................................. 1

## CHAPTER 1: Overview .................................................. 3
- Rationale .................................................. 3
- Collaborative Relationships .................................................. 4
- The Intervention Process .................................................. 4
- Resources During Planning and Implementation .................................................. 5
- Conclusion .................................................. 7

## CHAPTER 2: Getting Started .................................................. 9
- Request for Assistance .................................................. 9
- Before Intervention Planning .................................................. 16
- Conclusion .................................................. 30

## CHAPTER 3: Designing an Intervention With Informal Collaboration .................................................. 31
- Getting Started .................................................. 33
- Summarizing Responsibilities .................................................. 35
- Scheduling Immediate Follow-Up .................................................. 35
- Implementing the Plan .................................................. 36
- Providing Follow-Up .................................................. 38
- Conclusion .................................................. 40

## CHAPTER 4: The Structured 25 Minute Intervention Planning Process .................................................. 41
- Completing Preliminary Steps .................................................. 43
- Completing Step 1: Background .................................................. 46
- Completing Step 2: Problem and Goal .................................................. 48
- Completing Step 3: Responsible Behavior and Irresponsible Behavior .................................................. 50
- Completing Step 4: Consequences .................................................. 53
- Completing Step 5: Proactive Strategies .................................................. 55
- Completing Step 6: The Proactive Plan .................................................. 56
- Completing Step 7: Final Details .................................................. 58
- Providing Follow-Up .................................................. 64
- Conclusion .................................................. 66

## CHAPTER 5: The In-Depth Intervention Decision Guide (IDG) Process .......... 67
- Completing Preliminary Steps .......... 69
- Beginning the Planning Meeting .......... 70
- Completing Stage 1: Background .......... 71
- Completing Stage 2: Preparation .......... 81
- Completing Stage 3: Intervention Design .......... 88
- Completing Stage 4: Implementation .......... 96
- Providing Long-Term Follow-Up .......... 98
- Conclusion .......... 99

## CHAPTER 6: Skills of the Interventionist .......... 101
- Communication and Interpersonal Skills .......... 101
- Self-Evaluation and Reflection .......... 111
- Conclusion .......... 114

## CHAPTER 7: Creating a Climate for Collaboration .......... 115
- Developing Policies That Support Collaboration .......... 115
- Providing Ongoing Staff Development .......... 121
- Removing Roadblocks to School-Wide Collaboration .......... 121
- Inviting Staff to Use Collaborative Services .......... 126
- Conclusion .......... 127

References .......... 129

Reproducible Materials

# How to Use *Interventions*

*Interventions* is both a process and a resource for education professionals seeking to teach at-risk students the skills and attitudes needed to find greater success in the school setting.

The program materials include:

- **The *Interventions Procedural Manual***

    This manual provides information on the intervention process—how to design and implement high quality intervention plans.

    - **Chapter 1: Overview** includes a description of the "interventionist," an overview of the intervention process, and a quick reference guide to the 16 intervention booklets.

    - **Chapter 2: Getting Started** describes the initial request for assistance and preliminary steps to intervention planning. How are requests for assistance made? How are families involved? Which intervention process might be the best for different situations?

    - **Chapter 3: Designing an Intervention With Informal Collaboration** provides information on the role of informal collaboration in the intervention process. Informal collaboration occurs when professional assistance is easily accessible and staff members readily ask one another for suggestions and support.

    - **Chapter 4: The Structured 25 Minute Intervention Planning Process** describes a step-by-step intervention planning process. This process is particularly useful when working on a minor to chronic problem, and sometimes a severe problem in its early stages. How can intervention planning be structured so that planning is effective, but meetings do not drag on and on?

    - **Chapter 5: The In-Depth Intervention Decision Guide (IDG) Process** provides information on developing and implementing a comprehensive intervention plan using the "Intervention Decision Guide" ("IDG") form. This in-depth process is important when dealing with students who have chronic to severe problems. What background information is needed to develop an effective intervention plan? What are the goals and desired outcomes for the intervention? What intervention(s) might be appropriate? How is the intervention planned and implemented, and what is needed for follow-up?

    - **Chapter 6: Skills of the Interventionist** describes skills for providing support to other professionals. What issues should the interventionist be aware of? How can the interventionist engage in self-evaluation and reflective practices? How can the interventionist assist teachers when stress creates barriers to effective intervention?

    - **Chapter 7: Creating a Climate for Collaboration** provides information on how to build school-wide programs. How can school-wide programs encourage staff members to seek assistance through collaborative structures? How can school-wide programs guarantee that intervention planning will occur when necessary? How can school-wide programs remove the common roadblocks to collaboration?

- **Sixteen Intervention Booklets**

    These self-contained booklets provide step-by-step information on setting up and implementing sixteen specific interventions. The booklets can be used to increase knowledge in designing and carrying out specific intervention techniques and can be loaned to staff members who will be implementing the specific procedures. *Interventions* includes booklets for:

- Intervention A: *Managing Physically Dangerous Behavior*
- Intervention B: *Managing Severely Disruptive Behavior*
- Intervention C: *Planned Discussions*
- Intervention D: *Academic Assistance*
- Intervention E: *Restructuring Self-Talk*
- Intervention F: *Signal Interference Cueing*
- Intervention G: *Mentoring*
- Intervention H: *Self-Control Training*
- Intervention I: *Goal Setting and Contracting*
- Intervention J: *Teaching Desired Behaviors*
- Intervention K: *Self-Monitoring*
- Intervention L: *Structured Reinforcement Systems*
- Intervention M: *Managing Stress*
- Intervention N: *Classroom Management Strategies*
- Intervention O: *Increasing Positive Interactions*
- Intervention P: *Borderlines and Consequences*

- **Audio Tape Album**

    This optional 20 cassette collection provides entertaining and practical tips on how to use *Interventions*. Four tapes provide detailed information on how to fill the role of interventionist. Sixteen tapes describe the specific program interventions and can be used to highlight their main steps—an easy way to become acquainted with their procedures and to review their uses.

*Interventions* is designed for use by both individual interventionists (administrators, counselors, resource teachers, school psychologists, peer coaches, etc.) and collaborative problem-solving teams (Student/Staff Support Teams, Teacher Assistance Teams, Prereferral Teams, Child Study Teams, Intervention Planning Teams, etc.).

Elementary and secondary level scenarios have been woven throughout the *Interventions* program to illustrate how intervention strategies might be used in specific situations; however, every student, age level, and situation is unique. Ideally, you will create your own scenarios as you think of ways that these strategies might be used to help the students and staff you serve.

# CHAPTER 1

## Overview

### Rationale

DUE TO MANY factors, classroom teachers in America seem to be dealing with more and more at-risk students. Some are chronically angry and hostile; others are apathetic and withdrawn. Some students are insecure and need continual reassurance; others seem to be perpetually disruptive. Unless their problems are addressed, these students leave the school system still hostile, still apathetic, still insecure, and often still disruptive—ill-prepared to function productively in society.

Teachers usually understand the serious long-term effects of behavior problems and always recognize the immediate deleterious effect that one of these students can have on a classroom of twenty-five to thirty students. With more than one at-risk student in a class, the magnitude of these problems seems to increase exponentially. "Tom is a powerhouse—a leader, but he leads the class in the wrong direction. He gets Joe and Alicia going, and before I know it the three of them have the whole class into negative behavior and sarcasm." Because severe and chronic problems affect the whole classroom, intervention is needed for everyone's sake, not just the student with problems.

Given the increasing challenge posed by at-risk students, the individual classroom teacher cannot be expected to have all the answers. For some teachers, the isolation of the classroom leads to a sense that there are no solutions. "I've tried everything. The kid's got a problem and there isn't anything more that I can do. He needs to be removed from the classroom." For other teachers, asking for help feels like an admission of weakness or failure. "If I admit I don't have all the answers, my colleagues may think I'm not a good teacher." Neither view is productive. Teachers who feel they are on their own when dealing with problems are in an untenable position.

As schools intensify their efforts to bring all students into the educational mainstream, schools must create and foster an atmosphere of support and collegiality. Educators must pool and share their expertise to create effective interventions.

## Collaborative Relationships

*Interventions* is a resource guide for school personnel organizing to collaboratively develop high quality interventions for students at risk. The intervention process helps teachers, administrators, other educators, and family members combine their knowledge and resources to help students become responsible, self-directed individuals.

Collaboration occurs when two or more people work together to resolve a problem. Any teacher, specialist, or administrator who assists another staff member is an "interventionist," such as:

- A co-teacher, mentor teacher, or peer coach who works with another teacher to resolve classroom problems.
- A special educator who assists a classroom teacher with a mainstreamed special education student.
- An administrator who helps a classroom teacher develop a proactive plan for a student who is repeatedly referred to the office.
- A school psychologist who helps design a prereferral plan.
- A school nurse who doubles as the school's at-risk coordinator.
- A counselor who jointly develops plans with a teacher, student, and family to improve school success.
- Members of Teacher Assistance Teams, Student/Staff Support Teams, Student Study Teams, or Prereferral Teams who work together to develop formal intervention plans for at-risk students.
- Members of grade level planning groups, departmental groups, or mixed grade level groups assisting team members as they formally or informally develop strategies for resolving classroom problems.

## The Intervention Process

Whether implemented one-to-one with a teacher, or in a team problem-solving structure, the intervention process generally follows the sequence shown in Figure 1-1.

# Chapter 1
## Overview

### Figure 1-1: The Intervention Process

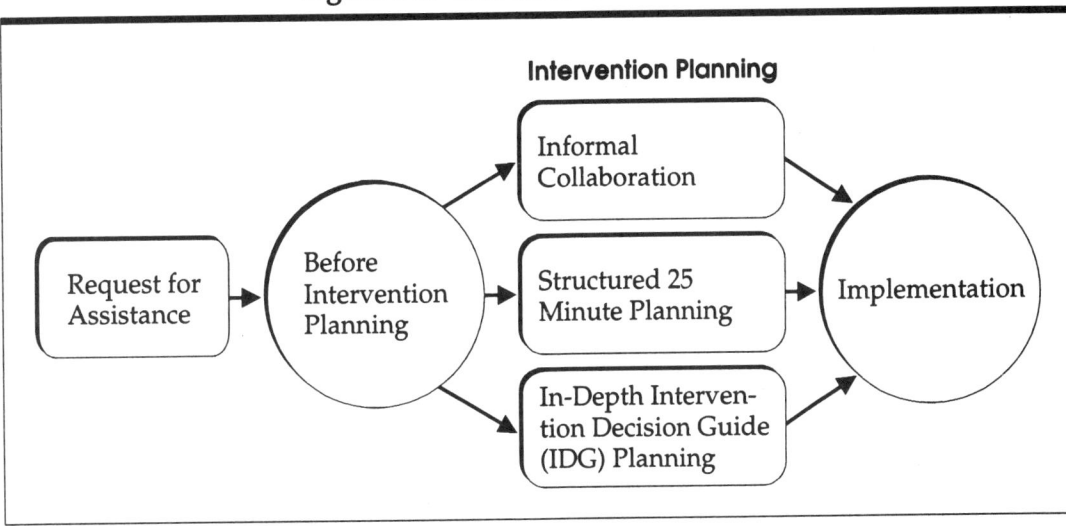

The intervention process begins with a request for assistance. The interventionist first helps the referring teacher with preliminary steps that need to be considered prior to intervention planning. Preliminary steps include determining the severity of the problem; involving the student and family in problem solving; obtaining parental permission for services when necessary; and deciding whether the situation calls for informal collaboration, a structured 25 minute planning process, or in-depth planning using the "Intervention Decision Guide" ("IDG") form.

Once the preliminary steps have been taken, an intervention plan is developed through an informal collaboration format, the structured 25 minute problem-solving format, or the in-depth format using the "IDG." During intervention, the collaborative group considers implementing a variety of procedures using the sixteen intervention booklets and their own knowledge and experience as resources.

The intervention plan is then implemented and evaluated. Over time, the plan is maintained, modified, or faded based on student success and progress towards goal(s).

## Resources During Planning and Implementation

To assist in planning and implementation, the intervention booklets provide detailed information on sixteen major interventions. Each booklet begins with a review of the steps that should be taken before implementing the procedure, a summary outline of the steps involved in the intervention, a detailed description of each step—along with an optional scenario to illustrate how the procedures are applied, and reproducible materials to use for note taking and implementing the intervention.

The sixteen program interventions are as follows:

- *Intervention A: Managing Physically Dangerous Behavior* provides information on establishing a temporary plan to deal with a student who is a threat to physical safety.

- *Intervention B: Managing Severely Disruptive Behavior* assists a teacher in developing an immediate plan to reduce behavior that is not physically threatening, but that prevents the teacher from teaching. This intervention assists teachers when dealing with problems such as overt defiance, flagrant disrespect, loud sustained disruptions, screaming, or aggressive behavior.

- *Intervention C: Planned Discussions* provides information on how to conduct a discussion and develop an informal action plan with a student. This process is useful with minor but potentially annoying misbehavior, moderate misbehavior in the early stages, and chronic or severe problems as part of a total plan.

- *Intervention D: Academic Assistance* provides information on how to conduct an informal academic assessment and how to adapt assignments and instruction to assist students in improving academic progress. This intervention is appropriate when students are struggling academically or have behavior problems that may be associated with underlying academic problems.

- *Intervention E: Restructuring Self-Talk* helps students learn to redirect negative thoughts about themselves or outside events. It is designed to assist students with problems such as negative attitudes, self put-downs, poor self-esteem, defeatist attitudes, self-control problems, and excessive criticism or sarcasm.

- *Intervention F: Signal Interference Cueing* teaches students to redirect or stop their inappropriate behavior by becoming aware of impulsive or habitual behavior. This intervention is useful with behaviors such as swearing, noncompliance, talking out, noise making, off task behavior, whining, complaining, and masturbating.

- *Intervention G: Mentoring* pairs a student with a caring adult in a one-to-one relationship. It is designed to assist students with problems associated with neglect, deprivation, lack of positive role models, lack of positive interactions with adults, poor self-esteem, conflict with authority, or the need for a positive relationship with an adult.

- *Intervention H: Self-Control Training* is an intensive plan that involves daily individualized lessons. Students learn how to recognize things that set them off and how to engage in alternative behavior. This intervention is designed to assist students with problems such as tantrumming, physical aggression, out-of-control anger, and chronic crying.

- *Intervention I: Goal Setting and Contracting* provides procedures for helping students identify achievement targets and specific actions that can be taken to reach those targets. This intervention is designed for students who need to become motivated, who need direction, and need to learn how to direct themselves. It can be useful with any problem, but is particularly useful when students lack responsibility, have negative attitudes, have few positive role models, conflict with authority figures, or seem to feel that they have no control over what happens.

- *Intervention J: Teaching Desired Behaviors* provides a detailed plan for teaching a behavior or strategy that can replace inappropriate behavior. It is designed to assist students with problems associated with poor peer relations, chronic off task behavior, problems interacting with adults, anger management, aggressive behaviors, or bad habits.

- *Intervention K: Self-Monitoring* helps students become aware of problem behavior and/or the improvements they are striving to make. This intervention helps students notice when they're engaging in inappropriate behavior so they can make other choices. As students learn to take control, they also begin developing pride in their accomplishments. This intervention helps students with mild misbehavior or habitual behavior such as blurting out, complaining, off task behavior, careless work, poor listening skills, making inappropriate comments, or poor social skills.

- *Intervention L: Structured Reinforcement Systems* provides unmotivated students with an incentive to improve their behavior through the use of a carefully designed system of external rewards. Providing a reinforcement system is a highly intrusive intervention that may be necessary when problems have been resistant to simpler solutions. It is designed to assist students with problems associated with work completion, quality of work, attendance, punctuality, and to help eliminate negative behavior such as disruptiveness, arguing, swearing, fighting, tantrums, and so on.

- *Intervention M: Managing Stress* provides a menu of stress reduction techniques. Sometimes a difficult student or students can heighten teacher stress, which in turn creates a barrier to effective intervention. This intervention helps teachers when they are feeling irritated, overloaded, fatigued, or frustrated.

- *Intervention N: Classroom Management Strategies* provides teachers with a menu of procedures that can help establish a safe, pleasant, and positive classroom environment. This intervention assists teachers with problems associated with management concerns, and includes strategies for assisting teachers who have students frequently referred to the office, parental complaints, or who have an especially difficult student or class.

- *Intervention O: Increasing Positive Interactions* establishes a plan for teaching students how to seek attention through responsible behavior rather than through misbehavior. This intervention can be very effective for students who seek attention through a variety of misbehavior ranging from excessive crying to disruptive behavior.

- *Intervention P: Borderlines and Consequences* helps teachers clearly define acceptable and unacceptable behavior and establish effective consequences when needed. This intervention is important when students "push the limits" and teachers find it hard to be consistent.

NOTE: *The audio tape album provides an optional resource for staff members who wish to become acquainted with the sixteen interventions.*

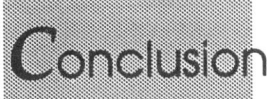

## Conclusion

For the purpose of clarity, the intervention process and intervention strategies are laid out sequentially; however, the step-by-step progression tends to fade as interventionists gain a thorough working knowledge of how to help at-risk students through the intervention process and potential intervention strategies.

# CHAPTER 2

## Getting Started

### Request for Assistance

THE INTERVENTION PROCESS begins with a request for assistance (see Figure 2-1). The request can be initiated in one of four ways: (1) a direct request is made by a staff member; (2) a student is automatically referred because of poor grades, detention, office referrals, or unexcused absences; (3) a student is identified as "at-risk" through early identification and screening; or (4) a request for assistance is made by a parent.

**Figure 2-1: Request for Assistance**

```
Request for  →  Before           →  Informal Collaboration         →  Implementation
Assistance      Intervention     →  Structured 25 Minute Planning  →
                Planning         →  In-Depth Intervention
                                    Decision Guide (IDG) Planning  →
                                 Intervention Planning
```

## Direct Requests By Staff Members

Direct requests for assistance are more likely to occur when they can be made either verbally or through a written referral process. Both avenues should be available to all staff members—teachers, teaching assistants, playground supervisors, specialists, administrators, and volunteers.

## Verbal Requests

Verbal requests for assistance occur naturally when the school actively promotes collaboration. Interventionists (i.e., counselors, school psychologists, administrators, resource consultants, and lead teachers) should let all staff members know that they are available to assist in joint problem solving.

**Principal:** *Drop in any time you think another head might help. No one is expected to have all the answers.*

---

**Mentor Teacher:** *Any time you want to talk about a situation or a particular student, I'm here. Problems are easier to solve early on.*

---

**Interventionist:** *How's Paul doing?*

**Teacher:** *I'm stumped. Could I bend your ear sometime?*

---

**Student's Former Teacher:** *I'm glad you've got Jennifer this year. She has many needs but she's a wonderful kid.*

**Student's New Teacher:** *I'm eager to find out what works with Jennifer. So far things are going pretty well, but I'd like to follow through on the things you started.*

When collaboration is viewed as a professional venture, staff members offer and seek assistance within the context of casual conversation. This leads to proactive plans to help students before misbehavior becomes a major problem.

**Teacher:** *Have you met Jacob Smith?*

**Interventionist:** *I haven't yet.*

**Teacher:** *He is very quiet, almost sullen. It's unusual for a young child. Lately, he's been making disrespectful comments like, "Sure, what are you going to do if I don't do my work?" So far he hasn't completely crossed the line, but he's edging right up to it.*

**Interventionist:** *Would you like me to do some checking on his background? It sounds like things could be heating up. We might be able to prevent a major problem.*

**Teacher:** *You bet. I'd like to get this resolved quickly.*

# Chapter 2
## Getting Started

## Written Requests

All staff members should be aware of and have access to a written referral system. Without the structure of a written procedure, some staff members may not think to seek help or may feel uncomfortable asking for assistance. If the staff is large, opportunities for casual contacts with interventionists may not present themselves. A written referral system can make the process easy and accessible for all staff members.

The sample "Informal Request for Assistance" form shown in Figure 2-2 allows staff to seek informal help when problems are still manageable, or more formal assistance when problems require structured intervention. To encourage assistance, referral forms should be placed near staff mailboxes.

**Figure 2-2: Informal Request for Assistance Form**

---

### Informal Request for Assistance

Date: 10/15
To: Matt Springer
From: Melissa Powell           Position: 2nd Grade Teacher
Re.: Bill Martin

**Brief description of the problem:**

Bill has been sent in from the playground for fighting twice this year. He is aggressive in the classroom and seems to have difficulty forming friendships.

☑ This is an informal request for assistance.
   (I'd just like some ideas at this point.)

☐ This is a request for formal assistance.
   (The problem may be serious enough for a structured intervention plan.)

---

*NOTE: A copy of this form is provided in the "Reproducible Materials" at the end of this manual.*

Some staffs may prefer to use a more detailed form as shown in Figure 2-3 for more advanced problems.

**Figure 2-3: Formal Request for Assistance Form**

## Formal Request for Assistance

| Referring Person | |
|---|---|
| Position | Date |
| Student | |
| Grade | DOB  /  /     Sex: ☐ M  ☐ F     IEP: ☐ Y  ☐ N |

**Check the Type of Problem Behavior**

| Academic: | ☐ Reading  ☐ Spelling  ☐ Writing  ☐ Study Skills<br>☐ Other_____ |
|---|---|
| Social: | ☐ Aggression  ☐ Noncompliance  ☐ Truancy  ☐ Tardies<br>☐ Withdrawal  ☐ Disruptions  ☐ Social Skills  ☐ Self-Management<br>☐ Other_____ |
| Communication: | ☐ Language  ☐ Fluency  ☐ Articulation  ☐ Voice<br>☐ Other_____ |
| Self-Help: | ☐ Dressing  ☐ Hygiene  ☐ Other_____ |
| Health: | ☐ Vision  ☐ Hearing  ☐ Physical  ☐ Other_____ |

**Provide a Specific and Observable Description of the Problem**

**Provide a Specific Description of the Problem Context**

Where:

When:

With Whom:

Other:

**Provide a List of Previous Remediation Attempts (If Any)**

1.
2.
3.

Source: Adapted with permission from Sugai, G.M. & Tindal, G.A. (1993). *Effective school consultation: An integrative approach.* Pacific Grove, CA: Brooks/Cole Publishing.

*NOTE: A copy of this form is provided in the "Reproducible Materials" at the end of this manual.*

# Sign-Up Books

Some staffs may also wish to provide the option of signing up for assistance in an appointment book (see Figure 2-4). The appointment book can be kept in the staff room or in a designated staff mailbox.

**Figure 2-4: Sample Sign-Up Book Sheet**

---

**Sign-Up for Intervention Planning Team Meeting**

**Note:** The team meets every Wednesday for one hour and addresses two situations. Sign up for the next available time slot. One of the team members will contact you before the meeting to confirm the time and to learn more about the nature of the problem. To protect the confidentiality of students, please sign your name only.

November 4, 2:45-3:15 _____

November 4, 3:15-3:45 _____

November 11, 2:45-3:15 _____

November 11, 3:15-3:45 _____

November 18, 2:45-3:15 _____

November 18, 3:15-3:45 _____

November 25—This is the beginning of Thanksgiving break. Even we aren't crazy enough to meet at this time!

December 2, 2:45-3:15 _____

December 2, 3:15-3:45 _____

If you want to meet with someone prior to an available time slot, be sure to talk to one of us or fill out a "Request for Assistance" form. You can leave it in Josie, Harry, or Victor's box, and they will get in touch with you as quickly as possible.

---

For additional information on how to foster staff readiness to request assistance, see Chapter 7.

## Automatic Referral Systems

Automatic or mandatory referral systems use preestablished criteria to identify students who need assistance. For example, a school may have a policy to consider intervention planning for students who have a certain number of unexcused absences or tardies, a specified number of discipline referrals, or failing grades. Automatic referral ensures that students receive attention even if staff members do not initiate a request. When automatic referral systems are used, the staff must be fully informed of the procedures so that the interventionist is not considered to be a "busy body."

## Referral Through Early Identification

The services of an interventionist may also be the result of an early identification process. Early identification procedures are implemented so that staff can intervene before students develop well-established patterns of inappropriate or antisocial behavior. One example of this process is *Systematic Screening for Behavior Disorders* (*SSBD*) (Walker & Severson, 1992) which provides a precise set of procedures for identifying students who are likely to develop social or behavioral problems. Once a student has been identified, staff can implement plans that encourage responsible behavior and prevent severe problems from developing.

## Parental Request

Occasionally the services of an interventionist are requested by a parent or guardian, either verbally or in writing. If this occurs, there is probably some element of dissatisfaction with the teacher. Due to the potential awkwardness of the situation, consideration should be given to sharing the problem with the building administrator. Because situations vary, professional judgment is required to determine how to best handle the parental request for assistance. In any event, action should be taken before the situation worsens. Two possible options include: (1) the building administrator might contact the parent to determine whether it would be reasonable for the parent to talk directly with the teacher before anything else is done; or (2) the administrator might talk with the teacher to see whether assistance is wanted or needed. The goal of the administrator and/or interventionist is to work with all parties to find common ground.

## Responding to Requests for Assistance

Because requests for assistance can be initiated in a variety of ways, the interventionist should use professional judgment in determining how to guide staff members through intervention planning:

- When a staff member makes a direct request for assistance, the interventionist generally helps the teacher determine the nature of assistance and the amount of assistance he would like.

  Interventionist: *I got your note about Rita. It sounds like you're worried. Tell me what's happening.*

  Teacher: *I'm not really sure yet. She's been on a crying binge all day long.*

  Interventionist: *Has this happened before?*

  Teacher: *She's one of those kids who hasn't spent time away from mom, so I know she's going through an adjustment period. I had hoped that by now she would be over it. Unfortunately, it seems to be worse.*

  Interventionist: *What have you tried so far?*

  Teacher: *I've talked to Rita and her mom, but I don't seem to be able to get any answers. Rita just says she's sad and her mom says that she is always this way when she is away from her.*

  Interventionist: *What direction do you want to go? I'd be glad to observe Rita, or we could do some intervention planning.*

- When referral has been through an automatic process, interventionists should be gently directive about the type of assistance that will be given.

# Chapter 2
## Getting Started

> Interventionist: We've been watching office referrals and noticed that Amy has been spending a lot of time in the office. I was wondering if you could help us figure out what's going on.
>
> Teacher: The kid is out of control. She has been harassing the other children—chasing them around the room. She laughs hysterically over nothing. I think she just wants attention.
>
> Interventionist: It sounds like Amy needs some help. I appreciate your filling me in. I'd like to talk more about this so we can figure out what to do.

- When the request for assistance is made by a parent, the interventionist must be sensitive to everyone's needs—the student's, parent's, and the teacher's. The interventionist will need the teacher's assistance in defining the problem and, if appropriate, eventually to assist with intervention planning. A focus on goals for the student and active problem solving may help the interventionist facilitate communication and resolve tensions.

> Interventionist: Mary, this is a little awkward, but the Bakers have called school. I'm sure that you are aware they are concerned about Amory's progress this year. What do you see as the problem?
>
> Teacher: I've been on the phone with them constantly. I'm not sure what to do. It really makes me angry that they called you, too.
>
> Interventionist: I can understand that. I thought we might work together to see if we could take some of the pressure off.
>
> Teacher: I don't know what you can do. I've got that awful class that everyone's been talking about. Amory is part of the problem.
>
> Interventionist: I know. The planets are in the wrong position for you this year or something. Tell me a little more about what's going on.
>
> Teacher: I think this group really lacks values. They don't seem to care about anything.
>
> Interventionist: Can you give me some examples of the problems?
>
> Teacher: Tons . . . .
>
> Interventionist: You're right. They're a challenging group. It's clear from what you've said that a lot of things just don't work. As you were talking, I had some thoughts. I know you've tried just about everything to this point, but there may be a few tricks left. First, I'd like to schedule an observation. Then, we can sit down to do some brainstorming and take a look at a menu of strategies we might consider. I don't want to leave you alone with this. If nothing else, I can begin running interference for you with the Bakers. I

know that you all want the same thing—it's a matter of trying to find a means to the end that actually works with this group.

Teacher: I don't think anything is going to work.

Interventionist: Nothing may, but if we work together we may come up with something that's worth a try. I can observe tomorrow at 9:00 or 12:45. Then we can meet either after school, or I can try to arrange to have someone cover your class in the afternoon. Which times would be best for you?

## Before Intervention Planning

Prior to intervention planning, the interventionist helps the referring teacher with preliminary steps that may need to be completed (see Figure 2-5).

**Figure 2-5: Before Intervention Planning**

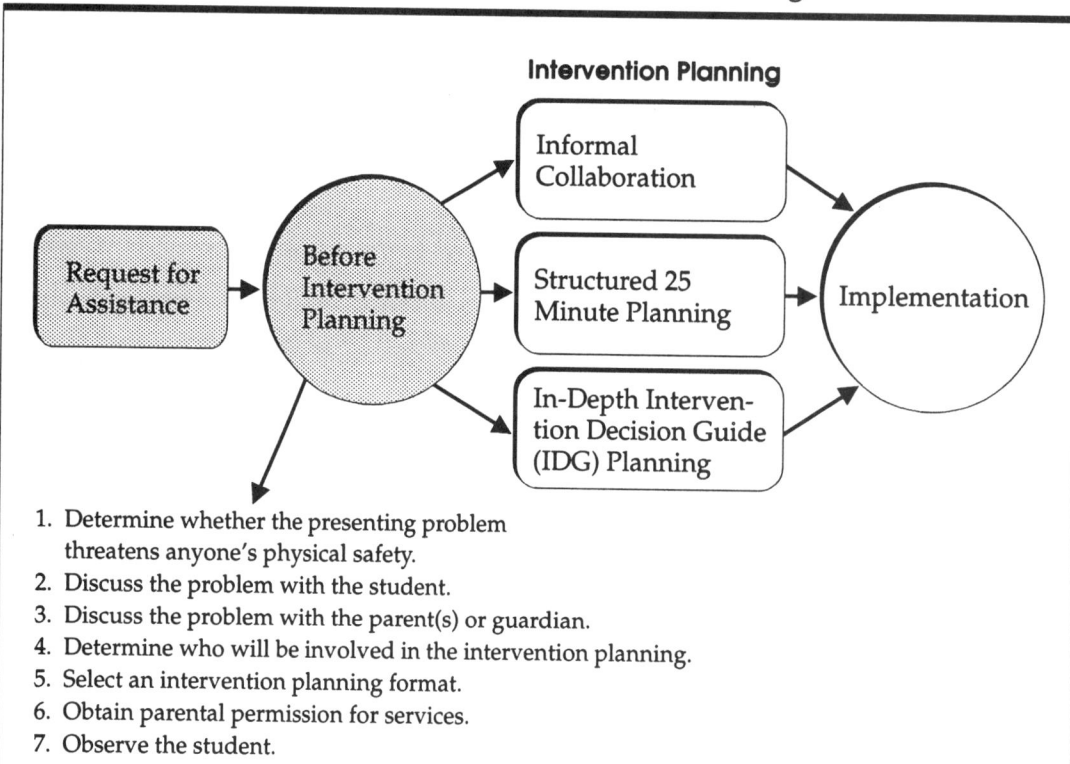

1. Determine whether the presenting problem threatens anyone's physical safety.
2. Discuss the problem with the student.
3. Discuss the problem with the parent(s) or guardian.
4. Determine who will be involved in the intervention planning.
5. Select an intervention planning format.
6. Obtain parental permission for services.
7. Observe the student.

1. Determine whether the presenting problem threatens anyone's physical safety.

If the student's behavior poses a physical threat, staff must act swiftly. Proceed immediately to Intervention A: *Managing Physically Dangerous Behavior*. This intervention includes five major components—implementing procedures to ensure everyone's safety, involving and notifying the student's parent(s) or guardian,

# Chapter 2
## Getting Started

17

developing record-keeping and reporting procedures, considering special education referral, and initiating long-range planning to teach the student to manage his or her own behavior.

> Mrs. Soo, a middle school teacher, has asked the counselor for assistance with Mack. Though it is only the second week of school, Mrs. Soo is worried about Mack's behavior.
>
> Teacher: *I think I may need some assistance with Mack. It's so early in the year and already he's creating problems. Someone bumps into him accidentally and he shoves back. Someone says something to him and he calls them names. Today, I asked him to make a correction on his math paper and he tore it up. He seems to be very impulsive and angry.*
>
> Interventionist: *Do you think he presents a danger to anyone?*
>
> Teacher: *No. He is physical, but I don't see him assaulting anyone.*

2. Discuss the problem with the student.

   Determine whether the teacher has had a one-to-one discussion with the student regarding the problem. If not, and the problem is mild, suggest that the teacher set aside a neutral time to simply discuss the problem. In the early stages, a student may not recognize the problem. Frequent verbal reprimands may have become so routine that the student doesn't take them seriously. The goals of a discussion are to: let the student know that the problem exists; convey the importance of finding a resolution; and communicate the desire to support and assist the student. (If a structured discussion is warranted, see Intervention C: *Planned Discussions*.) Though discussions may not resolve a problem, they should be considered prior to intensive intervention efforts.

3. Discuss the problem with the parent(s) or guardian.

   Determine whether the student's parent(s) or guardian have been contacted. If not, suggest that the teacher call or set up a conference with the parents. Contact should be made at a neutral time, not immediately following an incident. The purpose of the contact is to: inform the parents of the concern; communicate the school's desire to assist the student; learn more about the student from the parents; and to work with the family to establish joint goals and efforts to create a successful school experience.

   Families should be brought into the problem-solving process as early as possible. Early contact may result in an early resolution. Even when problems require in-depth planning, early communication with families establishes a foundation of cooperation and mutual respect. Parental assistance may be lost if contact occurs after a situation has reached crisis proportions. Many parents would be justifiably angry if they were informed of a problem after a formal intervention process had already been initiated. Families must be honored and treated with respect at all times. Cooperation can only be achieved through clear communication.

> **Interventionist:** You're right. It's awfully early in the year to see problems developing. Have you had a chance yet to have a discussion with Mack and with his parents?
>
> **Teacher:** Yes. The day Mack tore up his paper I kept him in during lunch break and talked with him. I didn't want it to be a punishment, just a time to see what was going on. Mack doesn't seem to be able to articulate the problem. He just shrugs his shoulders. Yet, I think he wants to please.
>
> **Interventionist:** How about his family?
>
> **Teacher:** I talked with his mom yesterday—Brenda Berringer. She seems nice. The parents have been divorced for three years. Mack may be caught in the middle. It sounds like the parents don't communicate at all. Brenda has Mack most of the time, although he stays with his dad some weekends. Brenda doesn't seem to know what to do. She says that school has been a problem since preschool. She even held Mack out of school an extra year to give him a chance to mature. She really wants this year to go better. She didn't have many suggestions for things we could do, but I think she would respond to help if we could offer it.
>
> **Interventionist:** I'm glad we're looking at this early. I'd like to set up a time to do some in-depth planning. Maybe we can get ahead of this and prevent a lot of heartache later.

4. Determine who will be involved in the intervention planning.

   Prior to intervention planning, the referring teacher and interventionist need to decide who will participate. If the referring teacher wants to informally discuss the problem and possible solutions, a one-to-one meeting with the interventionist may be appropriate. In other situations, planning may include family members, other staff members, and sometimes even the student. The size of the group will affect the planning process. The larger the group, the more time required for in-depth planning. However, increasing the size of the group also increases the sense of involvement in the plan.

   Several competing variables will determine who is to be involved. Consider the following questions:

   - *How severe is the problem?*

     If the problem is mild and the referring teacher is only requesting support and guidance, convening a large number of people for planning would be unwarranted—the proverbial making a mountain out of a mole hill. If this occurs, the referring teacher is unlikely to request assistance in the future. However, if the presenting problem is fairly severe, consider including all staff members who will take part in implementing the plan. For example, if the student is in middle school, all of the student's teachers might be invited.

# Chapter 2
## Getting Started

- *How available are people to meet?*

    Getting the ideal group of people together for planning may be an impossibility. If scheduling problems create delays, it is best to proceed with a smaller group. When this occurs, the interventionist will need to make arrangements to brief those not present at the meeting.

- *Who could provide important background information?*

    When problems are relatively serious, background information is necessary. In some situations, a former teacher may be able to suggest strategies that have worked with the student in the past. If the student has major difficulties on the playground, the meeting might include the playground supervisor. If the student receives the services of a specialist, the specialist should be included. The more knowledge the planning group has about a student, the greater the likelihood that the intervention can be tailored to meet the unique needs of the student.

- *Should family members be involved in the planning?*

    Family members should be involved in intervention planning whenever possible. They will be able to share their insights and experiences. Goals and expectations can be developed collaboratively, and the effectiveness of the intervention plan enhanced if parent(s) participate to whatever degree might be helpful to the student.

- *What type of planning group does the referring teacher prefer to work with?*

    The preference of the referring teacher should be a factor in determining who will take part in the planning. Some people prefer the support of a group, while others feel intimidated and prefer working one-to-one. Consider the size of the group and who would work well together.

- *What types of collaborative groups are already available to provide assistance?*

    The types of collaborative structures established in each school will also have an impact on the type of planning group that will be convened. Some schools have prereferral systems, Teacher Assistance Teams, Student Study Teams, Care Teams, Student/Staff Support Teams, At-Risk Teams, or some sort of multidisciplinary team.

When a request for assistance is made, the interventionist and referring teacher should determine who to involve in the intervention planning process.

---

Teacher: *Are you thinking about getting the Student Study Team involved?*

Interventionist: *We could; however, my inclination is to do the planning with you, maybe one or two of Mack's other teachers and his mother. We can go through the 'IDG' and develop a plan fairly quickly. What do you think?*

Teacher: *I have Mack for three periods plus homeroom this year. I think he has Karl for science and math, and Drew for P.E.*

> **Interventionist:** I'll check with Karl and Drew.
>
> **Teacher:** Good. Mack's mother might be intimidated if we refer this to the Student Study Team. I don't want to eliminate that option if we need other ideas later on, but I don't want Mack and his mother to feel that the staff is ganging up on them. In fact, maybe it would be best for just Mack's mother, you, and I to meet. Drew and Karl are always very supportive. I know they will cooperate with whatever we come up with.
>
> **Interventionist:** I agree. What about including Mack?
>
> **Teacher:** Of course we'll want to include him, but first I'd like to do some in-depth work with you and his mother. If Mack were there, I think we would be unable to talk freely.

5. Select an intervention planning format.

   Format options for designing an intervention include: informal collaboration, a structured 25 minute format, or the in-depth "Intervention Decision Guide" ("IDG") format. Figure 2-6 provides an overview of the three planning formats, and Chapters 3, 4, and 5 describe each process in detail.

# Figure 2-6: Overview of Intervention Planning Formats

|  | Informal Collaboration | Structured 25 Minute Planning | In-Depth Intervention Decision Guide (IDG) Planning |
|---|---|---|---|
| **Useful For:** | Mild misbehavior | Mild to moderate misbehavior | Moderate to severe misbehavior |
| **Participants:** | • Teacher and parent<br>• Teacher and interventionist<br>• Teacher, parent, and interventionist | • Teacher and parent<br>• Teacher and interventionist<br>• Teacher, parent, and interventionist<br>• Intervention planning team | • Teacher and interventionist<br>• Teacher, parent, and interventionist<br>• Intervention planning team |
| **Process:** | Unstructured and casual—a discussion of problems and possible solutions | A highly structured 25 minute planning session | A highly structured process that provides for in-depth planning |
| **Duration:** | • Informal stops with no time limit—may be as short as five minutes or as long as an hour | • Preestablished time limits<br>• Formal steps<br>• Recommended follow-up | • Formal steps with no time limit<br>• Thorough discussion of background<br>• Facilitates ongoing collaboration |
| **Pros:** | • Provides an opportunity for debriefing<br>• A few quick tips may help resolve a mild problem | • Time limits keep discussions focused<br>• Planning sessions do not go on and on<br>• The outcome is a specific, proactive intervention plan | • Has the highest probability for success<br>• Takes into account the multifaceted nature of problems<br>• Provides more support to the referring teacher<br>• Addresses severe problems |
| **Cons:** | • Can be too unfocused<br>• May spend too much time on extraneous details | • Time limits may make people uncomfortable<br>• May result in interventions too simple for complex problems | • May require a lot of time |

To select a planning format, consider how severe the problem seems to be, the nature of the situation, who will be involved in the planning session, and the styles of both the interventionist and the teacher.

The more severe the problem, the more structured the planning format should be. The "IDG" form is suggested for severe problems. Both the "IDG" or the 25 minute planning process will work for moderate to severe problems and either informal collaboration or the structured 25 minute planning process can be used for mild problems. Factors that reflect problem severity include:

- How intensive the problem behavior is;
- How intrusive the problem behavior is;
- How long the problem has been occurring;
- How resistant the problem has been to intervention; and
- Whether there is a long history of problems.

Use the descriptors shown in Figure 2-7 to help determine whether the behavior presents a mild, moderate, or severe problem. Categorization of the behavior is not intended as an evaluation. It will merely be used to determine which intervention planning format is most functional. Many problems will fall somewhere between categories (e.g., mild to moderate or moderate to severe). In that case, consider choosing the more structured approach.

**Figure 2-7: Categorizing Mild to Severe Problems**

| Mild | Moderate | Severe |
|---|---|---|
| • The teacher is concerned about a problem in its early stages.<br>• The student isn't motivated.<br>• The student is irritating or annoying, but doesn't interfere with instruction. | • The teacher is feeling very frustrated with the student.<br>• The student is always "pushing the boundaries."<br>• The student may not graduate.<br>• The problem has gone on for several weeks, despite discussions and mild verbal reprimands. Though the problem is relatively mild—whining, talking out, tattling, etc.—it is chronic or excessive. | • The student loses control and others are physically threatened.<br>• The teacher doesn't feel he or she can teach when the student has the problem.<br>• The situation is unfair to other students.<br>• The student has a long history of problems in many classrooms. |

Interventionist: *Mack's problem isn't severe yet, but it sounds like he has a history of problems. Normally, I'd suggest doing a quick intervention plan, but this time I'd like to use the 'Intervention Decision Guide.' It's a fairly involved process, but since Mack has already had a long*

> *history of school problems, we need an intensive intervention before inappropriate behavior escalates.*

6. Obtain parental permission for services.

   Prior to intervention planning, determine whether parental authorization is needed. If the student receives any services outside of the ordinary, including the services of a special education teacher, school psychologist, or collaborative problem-solving team, obtain parental permission. However, if collaboration occurs informally, parental permission may not be needed. If there is any doubt, err on the side of caution and courtesy.

   Permission to provide intervention should be requested initially by phone or in person, followed by written permission. School problems place parents in a difficult situation. Reactions range from anger to hurt to defeat. Some parents feel threatened while others feel protective. By talking with the parent prior to sending home a request for his or her written permission, questions can be answered and fears alleviated.

   > *Interventionist: I think it would be best if you set up an appointment with Mack's mom. I would like her to know that we'd like to contact Mack's previous school. It will help us save time. She should also know in advance that I'll be working with you.*
   >
   > *Teacher: I'll call this afternoon. She seems to be very bitter about Mack's past school experience, but I think she understands that I want to help and that I'm not out to nail him. I'll tell her that you will be helping—as an advocate. I'll try to let her know that you will be one more person that she and Mack can trust.*
   >
   > *Interventionist: Since the three of us will be working together, I don't think we need advance written permission. However, to be on the safe side, let's ask her to sign a permission slip. That way I can work with Mack whenever we feel it would be helpful.*

   A sample permission form is shown in Figure 2-8. Each staff should tailor parental permission forms to meet the requirements of their building and district.

Figure 2-8: Parental Permission Form for Intervention

# Parental Permission Form for Intervention

Dear ____Brenda____:

The staff of __Franklin Middle School__ strive to help all students feel a part of our learning community. Occasionally, we find that one of our students can benefit from additional assistance. We would like to provide __Mack__ with special support.

The goal of this assistance will be to help your child learn to:

__get along better with teachers and other students.__

Assistance may include, but is not limited to: reviews of the student's school file; informal academic assessment—reviewing work samples and habits, conducting an informal reading inventory; asking teachers about work habits and classroom behavior; classroom observations by a specialist; and the development of a supportive intervention plan developed by teachers and specialists in our building.

We need your permission to proceed with this assistance. Please sign the attached form and return it to __Mrs. Soo__ by __September 15__.

If you have any questions, feel free to call __Lilian Soo or the counselor, Mary Howard__ at __465-2211__ between the hours of __8:00 A.M. and 4:00 P.M.__.

We look forward to working with you and your child.

Sincerely,
Mrs. Soo

- - - - - - - - - - - - - - - - - - - - - - - - - - - - - - - - - - - -

### Parental Authorization for Student Assistance

Please check the appropriate box.

☐ Permission is granted to provide student assistance as described above.
☐ Permission is denied because _____
_____
_____

_____   _____
(Parent/Guardian Signature)              (Date)

NOTE: *A copy of this form is provided in the "Reproducible Materials" at the end of this manual.*

7. Observe the student.

   Prior to intervention planning it may be helpful for the interventionist to observe the student when problems occur most frequently. Settings might include the classroom(s), the playground, in the hallways, cafeteria, and on the bus.

# Chapter 2
## Getting Started

An objective observer can often see things that classroom teachers, playground assistants, or bus drivers cannot detect. Observers can watch for important details that may go unnoticed by professionals who have many responsibilities. For example, the interventionist may notice that a student always checks to see whether the teacher is looking when she misbehaves—a sure sign that the student craves adult attention. When observing on a bus, the interventionist may notice that the student is baited by other children—something the bus driver would not be able to monitor while driving the bus. The interventionist may observe that a student who has compliance problems always responds negatively when asked a question, but follows through when given a directive. These patterns may be important keys when deciding which interventions will have the highest probability of helping the student and teacher.

If the referring teacher and interventionist agree that an observation might yield important information, schedule a preconference meeting, the observation or observations, and a postconference meeting. Conferences can occur within the intervention process so that additional meetings are not required. For example, the preconference can occur when the initial request for assistance is made or when preliminary information is being gathered. The postconference can be arranged as part of intervention planning.

## Preconference

Before an observation, the teacher should be given clear information about the purpose of the observation and whether information from the observation will be confidential or whether it may be shared with the principal, an intervention team, or with parent(s). Being aboveboard at the outset can prevent hard feelings later on.

| | |
|---|---|
| Interventionist: | *Lillian, I think it might be helpful for me to observe Mack. Teachers have so much to do that there isn't time to just watch an individual student.* |
| Teacher: | *I think that would be okay.* |
| Interventionist: | *I'll be observing to see how Mack interacts with you and other students. We'll want to know how he responds during different activities in the classroom.* |
| Teacher: | *I should let you know that I get a little unnerved during observations.* |
| Interventionist: | *I understand. You might want to keep in mind that this is not a teacher evaluation. Our goal will be to see if there is anything we can do to help Mack. After the observation, we can determine what might be useful to share with Mack's mother.* |

The teacher and interventionist should both be aware that the student may not behave normally during an observation. Observers can change the climate of a classroom simply by being there. Some students will be on their best behavior, while others will act the same, or worse. If a student with chronic behavior problems is a perfect angel during an observation, the teacher may feel defensive. This is analogous to having problems with your car; only to have it run perfectly when the mechanic examines it. You invariably feel like an imbecile. "Really, it does make this weird noise when I'm driving it." To avoid feelings of discomfort, discuss in advance the likelihood that the observation may not yield a true picture of the student's behavior.

> Interventionist: *I know that kids sometimes act differently when I observe. Mack may be on his best behavior or he may behave even worse than normal. When we meet afterwards, I'll need your perspective. If you tell me his behavior was better than normal, we'll know what he is capable of. And, if it gets worse, we'll also know what he's capable of!*
>
> Teacher: *So, I should act as normal as possible too.*
>
> Interventionist: *Yes, but we'll also keep in mind that my presence may change things a bit.*

The teacher should know what the interventionist will be doing during the observation—taking notes, using any forms (see Figure 2-9), or taking data.

**Figure 2-9: Observation Form**

| \multicolumn{3}{c}{**Observation Form**} |||
|---|---|---|
| Student(s) | Teacher | |
| Date | Time | |
| Subject/Activity | | |
| **Time** | **Description of Student Behavior** | **Description of Teacher Interaction** |
|  |  |  |

*NOTE: A copy of this form is provided in the "Reproducible Materials" at the end of this manual.*

> Interventionist: *I'll be using a three-column 'Observation Form.' In the first column I'll record the time, in the second column I'll write down what Mack is doing, and in the third I'll describe what you do or say. Later, we'll look for interactional patterns. For example, some kids respond in certain ways to teacher directions or praise.*

Carefully work out the details of the observation process. During the preconference session, clear up as many procedural details as possible, such as:

- If the interventionist doesn't know the student, how will she recognize him without singling him out?

# Chapter 2
## Getting Started

> **Interventionist:** Lillian, I don't know Mack yet. Can you tell me how to recognize him?
>
> **Teacher:** Let me show you my seating chart. You'll also be able to recognize him physically. He is a good head taller than all of the other kids. He has dark brown hair and a stocky build.

- Will the interventionist be introduced to the class and if so, how?

> **Interventionist:** We should decide what we will tell the kids. If I just appear, there will be all kinds of questions and it may be disruptive.
>
> **Teacher:** Let me introduce you. Most of the kids already know you. We can tell them that one of your jobs is to watch kids at work.

- Will the interventionist talk to the target student and/or other students?

> **Interventionist:** I'd also like to tell the class that I'm going to need to concentrate on my job and that I won't be able to talk with them.
>
> **Teacher:** That's a good idea.

There are no right or wrong ways to handle situations that may occur during an observation; however, these questions should be addressed beforehand so the observation will not disrupt the class and teacher.

> **Interventionist:** I appreciate your being willing to let me observe.
>
> **Teacher:** I think it's a good idea. Now that you've explained what you'll be doing, and we've cleared up the details, I think it will be fine.

## Observation(s)

During the observation, follow the procedures that have been arranged with the teacher during the preconference. An anecdotal record of student behavior and teacher behavior (as previously described) can very useful. Figure 2-10 shows a sample of a completed "Observation Form." As indicated, the interventionist simply writes down the time, what the student does or says, and what the teacher does or says. This form can be used with an individual student, a group of students, or a whole classroom. The relatively open format allows the teacher and interventionist to look at a number of variables—approximate time on task and off task, the frequency of misbehavior, the duration of misbehavior, how the student responds to classroom events, and interactions between the teacher and student.

> Ms. Howard schedules a 9:30 A.M. to 10:00 A.M. observation for the next day. During the observation, Ms. Howard quietly observes and makes notes on the "Observation Form."

**Figure 2-10: Sample Completed Observation Form**

## Observation Form

| Student(s) | Mack Berringer | Teacher | Mrs. Soo |
|---|---|---|---|
| Date | 10/2 | Time | 9:30-10:00 |

Subject/Activity     Literature—small groups with teacher and independent work

| Time | Description of Student Behavior | Description of Teacher Interaction |
|---|---|---|
| 9:30 | Mack listens and gets out his materials | Teacher had students at desks get out SSR books. One group is called to the corner. |
| 9:32 | Starts whistling | No response |
| 9:35 | Listens to teacher and students in small group instead of reading. Loudly blurts out answer. | No response |
| 9:36 | Begins to fidget and tap pencil like a drum | "Jack, don't pound on your table. Get started on your reading." |
| 9:37 | Glares at the teacher, but opens his book and starts to read | No response |
| 9:39 | Gets out of his seat and gets a drink of water. Looks at teacher. Gargles loudly. | "Mack, that's not appropriate. Go to your seat and read." |
| 9:39 | Starts back to seat, but stops and pushes over a chair | Stares at Mack and motions him back to his seat |
| 9:40 | Gets back to his seat and opens book | No response |
| 9:43 | Continuing to read | Sends reading group back to their seats. Circulates and tells Mack that he is doing a nice job. |
| 9:47 | Gets out of seat and goes to pencil sharpener, but taps kids on the way | "Mack, keep your hands to yourself." |
| 9:50 | Blows up and yells, "Shut up. Leave me alone. I didn't do anything." | Looks away, conferences with another student |
| 9:51 | Takes seat, plays in his desk | No response |
| 9:54 | Takes out writing journal and begins drawing a picture | No response |
| 9:58 | Looks up but keeps drawing | Teacher calls Mack's group |
| 10:00 | Slowly picks up journal, puts it into desk, slowly picks up book, and walks slowly to group | "Mack, get to your literature group now." Looks exasperated. |

*NOTE: A copy of this form is provided in the "Reproducible Materials" at the end of this manual.*

# Postconference

The postobservation meeting can serve a dual purpose—to talk about the observation and to design the intervention plan. During the postconference, avoid making value judgments about the teacher or the classroom. As much as possible, keep the focus on the student, not on the teacher. Pay particular attention to the nature of the student-teacher interactions and any patterns that may be present.

To illustrate these guidelines, contrast the two postconference discussions following:

### Focus on Teacher Behavior (Incorrect)

Interventionist: *Lillian, during the observation I noticed that you pay a lot of attention to Mack when he misbehaves. Without realizing it you may be reinforcing his behavior by reacting to it. In fact, when he misbehaved and you didn't notice, he would get worse until you told him to stop. When you got mad, it really gave him what he wanted. Part of the intervention plan may need to involve changing the behavior you pay attention to.*

### Focus on Student Behavior (Correct)

Interventionist: *Lillian, Mack can be quite a handful. It seems like he is desperate to get attention—any kind of attention. Your attention appears to be very important to him; he often watches you, and if you are too busy to notice him, he gets worse. Do you get the sense that Mack seems to build up to an outburst and then calm down? If we observed for a longer period of time, I wonder if we'd see a real pattern emerge?*

Teacher: *Now that you mention it, he is very up and down. He does disruptive things, blows, and then is calm again. I never know what to expect.*

Interventionist: *This is valuable information. As we plan an intervention for Mack, we have some things to go on now. He seems to want attention, and he seems to have a pattern of gradually becoming agitated, blowing up, and then becoming calm.*

Information from observations can be very useful when designing an intervention. The objective view of the problem may increase the effectiveness of intervention planning and also provide important information for determining whether the student is making progress once the plan has been implemented.

## Conclusion

Collaborative planning tends to occur more frequently when procedures are in place to "get the ball rolling." Encouraging requests for assistance through informal and formal channels increases the likelihood that students and teachers receive help before a problem escalates. Once referral is initiated, the interventionist can help lay the foundation for effective intervention planning by working with the teacher, student, and parent(s) to gather important information and to select a workable intervention.

# Chapter 3

## Designing an Intervention With Informal Collaboration

INFORMAL COLLABORATION (see Figure 3-1) OCCURS when a staff member brings up a problem in casual conversation, or when a problem is relatively mild and the referring staff member is working through a period of trial and error—trying to find what works with a particular student or students.

**Figure 3-1: Informal Collaboration**

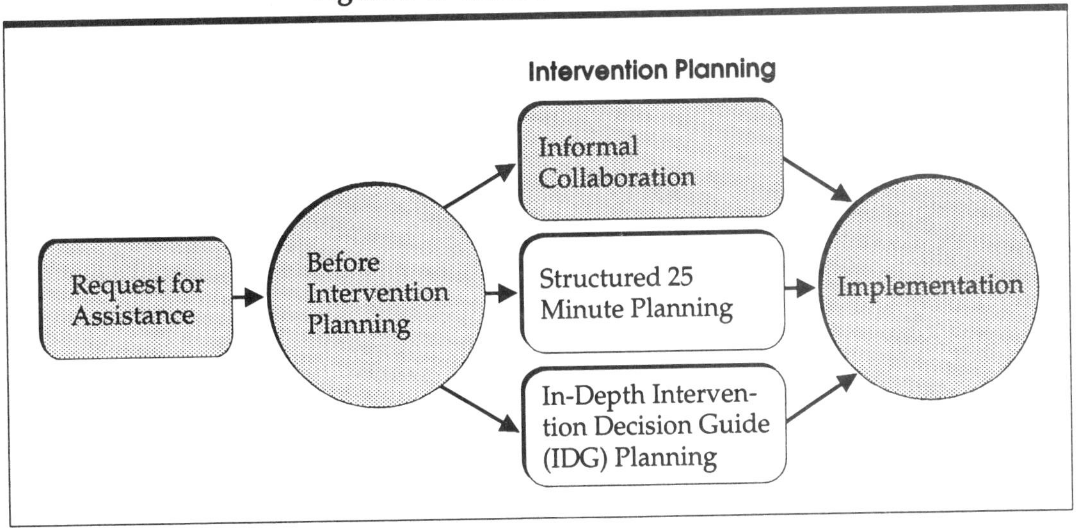

*Intervention Planning*

Request for Assistance → Before Intervention Planning → Informal Collaboration / Structured 25 Minute Planning / In-Depth Intervention Decision Guide (IDG) Planning → Implementation

Informal collaboration is generally useful for the following types of behavior:

- A staff member is concerned about a student.

    "I'm worried about Tina. She does fine in school, but she doesn't seem to have any friends."

- The behavior is irritating to a staff member.

    "Everytime I turn around, there's Eric wanting attention. He doesn't disturb anyone, but he has to be assured all the time that he's on the right track."

- The behavior is bothering other students.

    "Even the kids complain about Jenna's whining."

- The behavior tends to create a roadblock to success, but not consistently.

    "David just doesn't seem to care about his work; but, he does enough to get by. I hate to see him waste his potential."

Informal collaboration decreases the sense of isolation that a staff member may have when working on a day-to-day basis with hard-to-teach students. Because it is "informal," there are no procedures to follow. However, informal collaboration may serve a variety of functions:

- Staff members may need an opportunity to vent their frustrations.

    Teacher: *I hate to say it, but it sure would be easier if Danielle just stayed home once in awhile.*

- Staff members may need affirmation.

    Teacher: *Danielle threw a major tantrum today. It was really hard, but we all just carried on with our work.*

    Interventionist: *That's tough. You've done a terrific job of teaching your kids to ignore Danielle when she does blow. You've already helped her reduce the frequency of her tantrums and the duration.*

- Staff members may want another professional opinion.

    Playground Aide: *Lynette is a real puzzle. She is very quiet and withdrawn. At recess she just stands by the door. I'm worried about her. Do you think I should be?*

    Interventionist: *Tell me more about what's going on. She may need some assistance.*

- Staff members may want to look at possible solutions while problems are still relatively mild.

    Teacher: *Tad is always criticizing me and the other kids—to the point that the other kids are complaining. I've tried talking with him, but it doesn't seem to do any good. His mom says he does the same thing at home. Do you have any ideas?*

    Interventionist: *You know, something you might consider is signal interference cueing. Let me explain how it works, and then I'll give you a booklet to read. It might be worth a try. It's a relatively easy procedure to implement.*

# Chapter 3
## Designing an Intervention With Informal Collaboration

In some cases, informal collaboration may lead to the conclusion that a more structured problem-solving format would be helpful.

> Teacher: *Lisa almost bit one of the kids today. I had to restrain her.*
>
> Interventionist: *This sounds fairly serious. Has this happened before?*
>
> Teacher: *She's never tried to bite anyone before, but she is disruptive. I've taught for twenty years and I've never had a kid who was so hard to reach. I've tried being positive. I've tried using consequences, and nothing seems to work.*
>
> Interventionist: *I wonder if we ought to take a closer look at this. I would hate for it to get worse. Do you have time to talk with me this afternoon?*

Due to the range of situations that may prompt informal collaboration, outcomes vary. Informal collaboration may provide teachers with encouragement or an outlet for frustration. Informal collaboration may result in a list of possible solutions with no specific plans, or it may result in actual intervention plans that range from very simple to very complex.

Of the three planning formats included in *Interventions*, the unstructured nature of informal collaboration places the highest demands on the interpersonal skills of the interventionist. When discussing problems on an informal level, the interventionist needs to be able to determine whether the teacher just wants to talk or is actually looking for suggestions. The interventionist needs to know how to gently guide the discussion if it turns into a nonproductive gripe session; and if the situation warrants it, the interventionist needs to begin the process of exploring more structured intervention planning. (For additional information about the skills of the interventionist, see Chapter 6.)

## Getting Started

Informal collaboration may arise out of a direct request for assistance, via an automatic referral process, or through an early intervention process. Once the request for assistance has been made, the interventionist works quickly through the preliminary steps and assists with intervention planning.

In the following scenario, a playground supervisor talks with a classroom teacher about a student in her class. In this instance the teacher is serving as an interventionist—assisting another staff member with problem resolution.

> Playground Supervisor: *I have a terrible time with Rose on the playground. She is very disrespectful.*
>
> Teacher: *I'm sorry to hear that. Can you tell me what she does?*

**Playground Supervisor:** *If I remind her of a rule or give her a direction, she is very snotty. Today I reminded her that she was not supposed to walk up the slide and she said, 'You're not my teacher. You can't tell me what to do!' Then she got off the slide, but not without giving me a superior look.*

**Teacher:** *She was also a little mouthy with my substitute the other day.*

**Playground Supervisor:** *I had the same problem last year. Her teacher would talk to her and she would get better, but then she would be back at it within a few days. It's like a habit. She doesn't stop and think. She just reacts.*

**Teacher:** *I've never had problems with Rose, but she seems to have trouble with other adults. How would it be if we had a discussion with Rose? I think it would be helpful if you were involved. Rose needs to understand why you give directions, and how important it is to listen and be respectful.*

**Playground Supervisor:** *That would be okay with me.*

**Teacher:** *Maybe we could do some goal setting. I have a booklet that includes sample forms and describes a goal-setting process. First, we would all decide on a goal. Then, we would identify what Rose could do to meet the goal. For example, we might decide that she will respond respectfully to directions by nodding and following directions. We would also specify things that you and I would do to help. For example, I might do some role playing with the whole class and have everyone practice respectful responses to directions and corrections. We might have you give me a daily report, and maybe work out some sort of cueing system so that Rose can think about what she's doing. We can work out the particulars with Rose. I can loan you the goal setting booklet to skim through before we meet with Rose.*

**Playground Supervisor:** *That sounds good. I know it seems trivial, but I'm going to have Rose on the playground for the next three years. I don't like the other students to see her being so disrespectful.*

**Teacher:** *Let's figure out when we can meet with Rose. I'll also call her mother and let her know what we're doing.*

Even though the collaboration was informal, the teacher and playground supervisor have generated a fairly structured intervention plan.

# Summarizing Responsibilities

If an intervention plan is developed through informal collaboration, the interventionist can help ensure that the plan is implemented by summarizing everyone's roles and responsibilities. Due to the informal nature of the planning, the interventionist should use his or her professional judgment to determine whether a written summary would be useful and appropriate.

# Scheduling Immediate Follow-Up

Whether informal collaboration results in an actual intervention plan or not, follow-up should be scheduled:

- When the problem is only discussed and no intervention plan is developed, the interventionist should plan to follow up within a few days to see how things are going. Some interventionists make a simple notation in their calendars. "May 5—Check with Sophia to see how Gavin is doing."

- When informal collaboration results in an actual intervention plan, set up an immediate follow-up schedule. The follow-up schedule should include: a brief check-up that occurs within a day or two of implementing the plan, optional observations, and a follow-up conference that occurs after the first week of implementation. (Subsequent follow-up meetings can be scheduled at that time.)

    - The brief check-up provides an opportunity to iron out any problems. Plans can fail if something is forgotten or misunderstood. Sometimes they require immediate revision. The brief check-up provides a safety net to ensure that an ineffective or poorly implemented plan is not continued for a week or longer.

    - Optional observations provide an opportunity for an outside observer to see how the plan is working, and to determine whether any variables need adjustment.

    - The first follow-up conference allows the participants to evaluate the effectiveness of the plan.

> **Teacher:** *We'll meet with Rose on Monday during lunch to do the goal setting. Then I'll plan to be out during afternoon recess in case we decide to use signal interference cueing. We can show Rose how it works, and we can iron out any problems.*
>
> **Playground Supervisor:** *This sounds wonderful. The only thing I worry about is having it work for a week and then having her fall back into her old ways again.*

> Teacher: That's very likely, isn't it? We'll need to keep Rose focused on her goal of being respectful. Let's have lunch a week from Monday and we can assess where we are. Eventually, I think we can move to some sort of self-monitoring system. I can easily check with you once a week when I have duty.

## Implementing the Plan

During implementation, it is important for staff to follow through with their responsibilities. Plans often fail because the adults are not consistent and persistent. At-risk students are often used to plans that go nowhere. "Oh, yeah. They'll do that for a week or so, but then they'll forget about it. It's no big deal."

Commitment and consistency can make the difference in whether an intervention plan works or not.

> During the conference with Rose, the playground supervisor, and teacher use the goal setting form shown in Figure 3-2.

# Chapter 3
## Designing an Intervention With Informal Collaboration

### Figure 3-2: Goal Setting

**Short-Range Goals 1**

Name: Rose Gibbons   Date: 11/15   Grade: 3

My personal goal is: to learn to be respectful of others.

I can show that I am working on this goal by:

thinking about my actions and words on the playground. When Miriam gives me a direction or a correction, I need to stop what I am doing and listen. I need to follow the directions and acknowledge Miriam or any of the other playground supervisors by nodding. If I disagree with the direction, I need to follow the direction. After I count to fifty, I can politely ask about the direction.

**Student Signature**

I can help you reach your goal by:

working on this goal with our whole class. We will role play talking respectfully, following directions, and asking polite questions when we disagree. I will also check with you each day, and Miriam twice a week for the next two weeks to see how you are doing.

**Teacher/Mentor Signature**

I can help you reach your goal by:

modeling how to speak respectfully. I will use your name when I need your attention. When you listen politely and follow directions, I will acknowledge you with a smile or comment. When you have a question that is asked politely, I will answer back just as politely.

Playground Supervisor
~~Parent~~ **Signature**

Following the goal-setting conference, Rose's teacher and the playground supervisor agree that Rose responds well to positive interactions. In addition to following through with the goal contract, Rose's teacher and the playground supervisor decide to work on positive interactions. The teacher agrees to walk to recess with Rose twice a week, and the playground supervisor agrees to make it a point to say hello to Rose each recess.

# Providing Follow-up

The first follow-up consists of an initial "check-up" during or after the first day of implementation. Then another follow-up conference is scheduled after the first week of implementation. During each follow-up conference, subsequent conferences may be planned.

During the conferences, participants evaluate student progress and make modifications to the plan if needed. Evaluation should include two easy-to-implement procedures that will provide clear indications of whether the intervention is helping the student. Using two separate evaluation procedures tends to validate the results. One procedure can be as simple as asking the teacher how things are progressing. Other procedures include: counting a behavior; self-monitoring data; the student's own perceptions; information from a series of observations by the interventionist; data from a reinforcement system; information from observations by video or audio taping, such as frequency counts, or the length of time a student engages in a particular behavior; discipline referrals; records on assignment completion; and so on. (Specific evaluation procedures are suggested in each intervention booklet and are discussed in more detail in Chapter 5.)

Evaluation information helps determine whether the plan should be maintained, modified, or faded. General guidelines for maintaining, modifying, and fading plans include:

- Develop a new intervention plan if the student makes no progress or gets worse.

    When a student shows no progress, the plan may need to be redesigned. However, before abandoning a plan, there should be two independent means of verifying that the plan is not working. If a student has been making good progress, but "blows it" one day, a teacher may feel that the student hasn't made any progress at all. Evaluation information and the support of the interventionist can help the teacher and student stay on course.

- Modify the intervention plan to provide more support and structure if progress is very slow, or has come to a halt.

    Because intervention planning involves trial and error, it may become apparent that the student needs more assistance.

- Maintain the intervention plan if the student is making good progress.

    If the student is making steady progress toward a goal, the plan should be maintained until the student demonstrates continuous success in achieving the goal.

- Fade the intervention plan when there is a high probability that the student can maintain success.

    Fading is accomplished by gradually providing less structure and support. Some intervention plans are automatically faded as the student becomes successful. For

# Chapter 3
## Designing an Intervention With Informal Collaboration

example, use of visual reminders in signal interference cueing would be used less and less frequently as a student demonstrated success. Eventually, the cueing could be faded completely.

> Within the first week of setting up Rose's goal-setting contract, Rose, the playground supervisor, and her teacher meet to discuss her progress. In this plan, evaluation involves simply checking each participant's perceptions.
>
> **Teacher:** We are meeting again to see how Rose is doing on her goals and to determine whether our plan is working. You each have a copy of our original goal-setting form. Rose, you have worked very hard during the role playing that we've done in class. I think it's helped the whole class. What do you think Rose?
>
> **Rose:** Well, I think it's been fun.
>
> **Teacher:** Miriam, how do you think things are going?
>
> **Playground Supervisor:** I'm very pleased. Rose, when I say 'Hi' to you, I know that I'm going to get a wonderful smile. I enjoy seeing you at recess!
>
> **Rose:** Can I ask a question?
>
> **Teacher:** Yes, Rose.
>
> **Rose:** I won't get in trouble?
>
> **Teacher:** (Looks at Miriam, who nods.) I think you are being very responsible because you are thinking carefully about what you want to ask. Can you ask your question respectfully?
>
> **Rose:** I'll try. Miriam, I was wondering why you have to yell at us.
>
> **Playground Supervisor:** I do yell, don't I? You know Rose, I have a funny old voice. When I want your attention, if I talk loud enough for you to hear on the playground, it sounds like I'm yelling, but I'm not angry.
>
> **Rose:** Oh.
>
> **Teacher:** Rose, that was very mature of you, and Miriam, that was very gracious of you to answer Rose so honestly. Well, I think we all agree that you are doing extremely well with your goal Rose! I'd like to keep this plan up a bit longer. We might make one alteration though. Rose, would you like to continue role playing in our room once a week?
>
> **Rose:** Yes, but maybe about something else.

> Teacher: Great, maybe you and I can come up with a class goal that we could work on. Shall we all meet again in two weeks?

Follow-up not only allows an opportunity to evaluate student progress and make modifications as needed, but also provides all participants in the plan with continued support. Intervention plans are more often successful when a focus on the goals can be maintained. They tend to be only temporarily successful if abruptly forgotten. Even after an intervention plan has been faded, the interventionist should periodically check to see that satisfactory progress is continuing.

> Teacher: Since we aren't formally meeting on Rose's goal anymore, I thought I'd see how she was doing.
>
> Playground Supervisor: You know, she was doing really well, but she sure glared at me the other day. She didn't say anything though.
>
> Teacher: I think I'll do a little role playing again. We haven't done that in class for a long time and I really think it helps all the kids be aware of their behavior—toward everyone.
>
> Playground Supervisor: I appreciate that. I'm glad you brought this up. I need to make it a point to stay friendly with Rose. We've kind of dropped our old habit of saying hello to each other.
>
> Teacher: That's great. Rose's a neat kid, but since those disrespectful interactions have been ongoing for at least a year, it would be very easy for her to fall back into old habits. I'll check with you again next Wednesday to see how she's doing.
>
> (See the booklets Intervention I: *Goal Setting and Contracting*, Intervention F: *Signal Interference Cueing*, and Intervention O: *Increasing Positive Interactions* for more information on the strategies mentioned in this scenario.)

# Conclusion

When a problem is mild, or a referring staff member prefers a casual approach to problem solving, informal collaboration can be highly effective. However, the unstructured nature of this collaboration may decrease the clarity and efficiency of planning. Participants may wish to use the Structured 25 Minute Planning process or the in-depth "Intervention Decision Guide" ("IDG") process described in the next chapters.

# CHAPTER 4

# The Structured 25 Minute Intervention Planning Process

THE STRUCTURED 25 minute intervention planning process (see Figure 4-1) provides a timed, step-by-step format for developing an intervention plan. This format is appropriate when a systematic intervention plan would be helpful; and when a worthwhile plan can be developed within a time limit. The 25 minute process may be used by the interventionist and referring teacher for a mild to moderate problem. If the problem has been referred to an "intervention team" of some kind, the 25 minute process might be the first step in dealing with a moderate to severe problem. (If problems persist, more in-depth planning may be required through the use of the "Intervention Decision Guide." See Chapter 5.)

Figure 4-1: Structured 25 Minute Planning

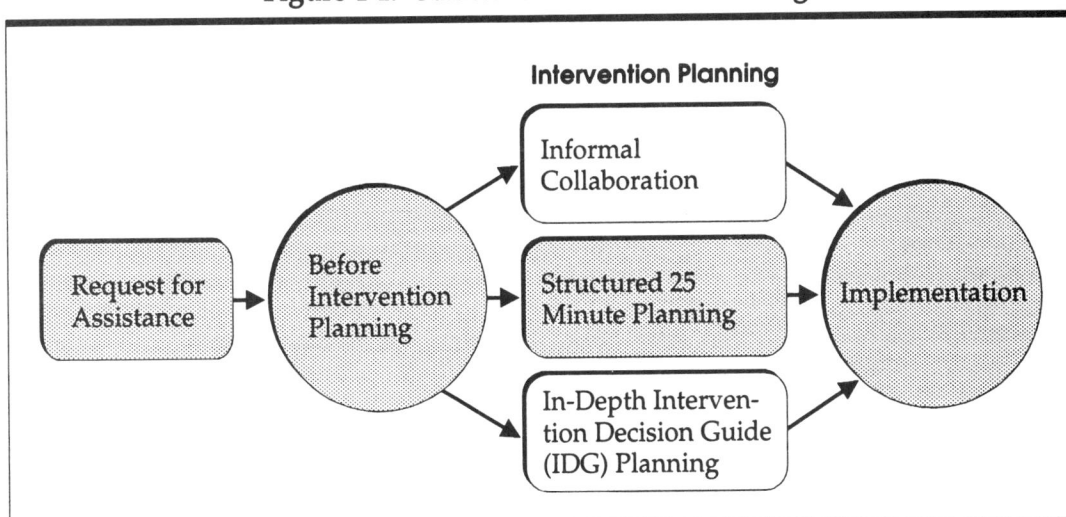

Figure 4-2 shows the two-page planning agenda for the 25 minute process and time limits for each step. (Larger illustrations of all the sections of this form will be provided throughout this chapter.)

Figure 4-2: Planning Agenda

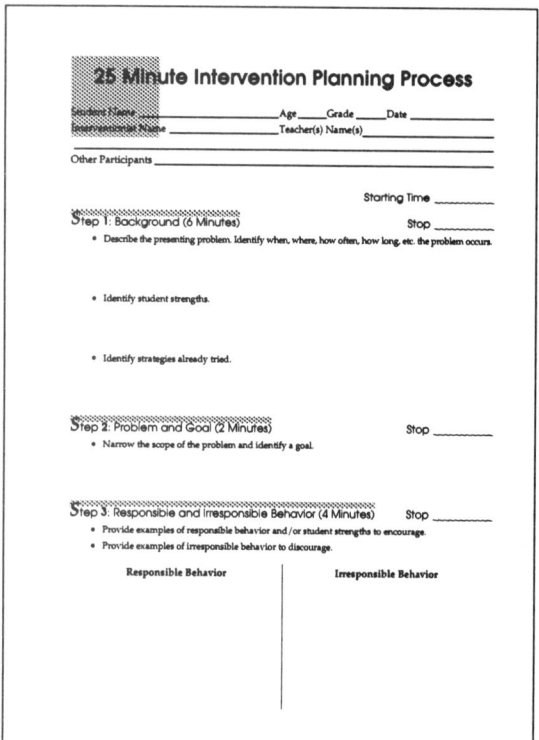
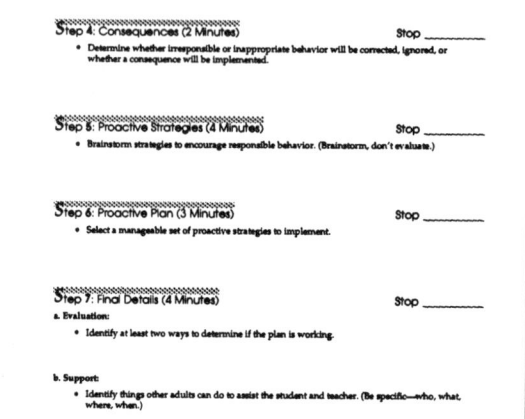

*NOTE: A copy of this form is provided in the "Reproducible Materials" at the end of this manual.*

Initially, 25 minutes may not seem like enough time. However, as interventionists or teams become proficient with the process, intervention planning can often be completed in less than 25 minutes. When first learning to use the 25 minute process, teams may wish to allow more time at each step as illustrated in Figure 4-3. Longer time limits allow collaborative teams the time that may be needed to learn how to complete each step in the process. Eventually, the interventionist or team will become proficient enough in the planning process to stay within the 25 minute structure.

# Chapter 4
## The Structured 25 Minute Intervention Planning Process

**Figure 4-3**

| Structured Intervention Planning | 25 Minute | 35 Minute | 50 Minute |
|---|---|---|---|
| Step 1: Background | 6 minutes | 7 minutes | 10 minutes |
| Step 2: Problem and Goal | 2 minutes | 3 minutes | 4 minutes |
| Step 3: Responsible and Irresponsible Behavior | 4 minutes | 6 minutes | 8 minutes |
| Step 4: Consequences | 2 minutes | 3 minutes | 4 minutes |
| Step 5: Proactive Strategies | 4 minutes | 6 minutes | 8 minutes |
| Step 6: Proactive Plan | 3 minutes | 4 minutes | 8 minutes |
| Step 7: Final Details | 4 minutes | 6 minutes | 8 minutes |

## Completing Preliminary Steps

Before intervention planning begins, the interventionist and referring teacher complete the following preliminary steps, detailed in Chapter 2:

1. The interventionist determines whether the presenting problem threatens anyone's physical safety. (If so, Intervention A: *Managing Physically Dangerous Behavior* should be immediately implemented.)
2. The interventionist determines that the teacher has discussed the problem with the student.
3. The interventionist or teacher informs the parent(s) (or guardian) of the problem, invites them to participate in problem solving, and obtains their permission for intervention planning.
4. The interventionist may conduct a student observation or observations.

| | |
|---|---|
| Interventionist: | *I got your note and thought we should set up a time to talk about Charlene.* |
| Teacher: | *Great. I need to bounce around some ideas. I'm not getting anywhere.* |
| Interventionist: | *Can you fill me in briefly so we can decide how to proceed?* |
| Teacher: | *It's hard to sum up, but I guess Charlene's overall problem is being disruptive and off task.* |
| Interventionist: | *Have you talked to Charlene and her parents?* |
| Teacher: | *Yes. Charlene always says she'll try, but nothing changes. Her mom just makes excuses and doesn't have any suggestions.* |

> **Interventionist:** Would her mom agree to our setting up a plan for her?
>
> **Teacher:** I think so. She's protective, but she wants the best for Charlene.
>
> **Interventionist:** Do you want this to go to the Child Study Team?
>
> **Teacher:** I don't think this warrants referral yet, but I do need some help.
>
> **Interventionist:** We could set up a time to meet and informally collaborate, or if you want we can follow a 25 minute planned agenda. Either way is fine.
>
> **Teacher:** With time as it is, I think I'd like to structure the planning. I have some time tomorrow afternoon before I go to a district meeting. The 25 minute format sounds good.
>
> **Interventionist:** If you can wait a day or two, I'd be happy to schedule an observation. Do you think it might be helpful to have me watch to see what she does during independent work times? I know that you are always interacting with your students. It must be hard to keep an eye on Charlene.
>
> **Teacher:** That would be great, but it will push our meeting way back. My schedule's really tight for the next week and a half.
>
> **Interventionist:** I hate to wait a couple more weeks. If we think it would be helpful, I can always schedule an observation later. We should let Charlene's parents know that we would like to develop a plan to help Charlene, and that I will be involved. Would you like her parents to join us?
>
> **Teacher:** I hadn't thought about it. I'll call Mrs. Metzger and sound her out.
>
> **Interventionist:** If she doesn't plan with us, you can tell her that I'll call and let her know what we've come up with. That way, I can make contact and she'll know that Charlene has both of us as advocates, not adversaries.

Prior to the planning meeting, the interventionist fills out the top of the form as shown in Figure 4-4. One copy is made for each participant. If time limits will be followed, the interventionist should decide how time will be kept. One method is to use a timer. When the timer goes off, a time keeper (the interventionist or someone else designated to be the time keeper) gently moves the group to the next step. A second method is to note when participants are ready to begin, note the start time, and quickly jot down stop times in advance for each step. (As shown in Figure 4-4, space is provided on the right side of the form to record the initial starting time and the stop times for each step.) If this method is used, the interventionist should use a stop watch, digital clock, or digital watch to monitor the time and guide the group to the next step. If the group completes a step faster than the designated time, the additional time can be used for the next step.

# Chapter 4
## The Structured 25 Minute Intervention Planning Process

**Figure 4-4**

### 25 Minute Intervention Planning Process

Student Name __Charlene Metzger__   Age __8__   Grade __3__   Date __11/18__
Interventionist Name __Maria Trent__   Teacher(s) Name(s) __Troy Winfrey__

Other Participants __Connie Metzger, mother__

Starting Time _____

**Step 1: Background (6 Minutes)**   Stop _____

- Describe the presenting problem. Identify when, where, how often, how long, etc. the problem occurs.

## Beginning the Planning Meeting

The interventionist (or referring teacher) convenes the meeting by setting the tone—welcoming each participant and establishing an atmosphere of support and advocacy for the student.

> **Teacher:** I'm glad that we could all meet. This is Connie Metzger, Charlene's mother, and this is Maria Trent, the school counselor. Maria often helps us develop plans for our kids.
>
> **Interventionist:** Thank you for coming, Connie. We're always glad to see parents and teachers working together. I'm looking forward to developing a plan to help Charlene. She's a delightful girl. I love her sense of humor.

If any of the participants are unfamiliar with the 25 minute process, the interventionist should explain the format and time limits before the intervention planning begins. If the planning format hasn't been jointly selected in advance, staff or family members may feel rushed or even railroaded into accepting an intervention plan. When possible, provide participants with the option of following the agenda within the 25 minute period, with extended time limits, or without time limits. If family members are involved, special precautions need to be taken so they feel that they've had the opportunity to fully participate. If participants decide to stay within the time limits, the meeting will move very efficiently. Without time limits, the meeting will be more casual and responsive to the needs of participants, but is also likely to last longer.

> Interventionist: Connie, we've decided to follow a 25 minute agenda. I know that you and Troy have already talked. The 25 minute format is kind of stiff, but we thought it would allow us to develop a plan for Charlene without waiting until we all have more time. Troy has another meeting at the district office in about 45 minutes. So, if it's okay with you, we'd like to do some fairly focused planning. Then, if you'd like, I can talk with you some more when Troy has to leave.
>
> Parent: That would be fine. I know Charlene doesn't like school this year, and I don't see her making good progress.
>
> Teacher: I'm excited about helping Charlene. I don't want her to feel like we are always complaining about her behavior. I'd really like to help.
>
> Interventionist: I appreciate everyone's cooperation. I'm going to record stop times for each step. Our estimated start time is 3:15. Then we'll have until 3:21 for Step 1, 3:23 for Step 2, 3:27 for Step 3, and so on. As we're talking, I'll try to gently guide us to the next step when our time is up. You can help me by also watching the time. My apologies in advance for the interruptions.

# Completing Step 1: Background

The interventionist begins the process by summarizing the problem, inviting all to participate, reiterating the proactive nature of the planning, and describing Step 1.

> Interventionist: When we first talked, Troy said that he was worried about Charlene because she had difficulty working independently. As we talk, we'll try to get a handle on the problem so we can develop a plan to help Charlene become more independent. Connie, please feel free to share your perceptions. In Step 1, we want to discuss the problem, Charlene's strengths, and also things that have been tried so far. Troy, why don't you begin by filling us in on what you see in the classroom?

During Step 1, the interventionist paraphrases, takes notes, and asks clarifying questions, such as:

- How often does she engage in the misbehavior?
- How long does the misbehavior last?
- Where does the misbehavior occur?
- Does she engage in the misbehavior in other settings—in P.E., on recess, in the hallways, or in the cafeteria?

# Chapter 4
## The Structured 25 Minute Intervention Planning Process

- Is the misbehavior more likely to occur during math, reading, independent work, or during instruction?
- How do the other students respond?
- What strategies have been tried to resolve the problem?

> **Teacher:** Charlene has the greatest difficulty during independent work times. I worry about her because she doesn't seem to be able to get anything done unless I'm standing over her. She wanders aimlessly about, sharpens her pencil, gets a drink of water, and often bothers the other students.
>
> **Interventionist:** How do the other kids respond to her?
>
> **Teacher:** They don't seem to mind her interruptions. Charlene is very likable. She has that good sense of humor.
>
> **Interventionist:** So, a problem is wandering and bothering other kids, but a strength is her social skills.
>
> **Parent:** Yes, Charlene has a lot of friends.
>
> **Teacher:** Everyone likes Charlene so she can pull them off task. She doesn't harass anyone.
>
> **Interventionist:** How does she do during instructional periods?
>
> **Teacher:** She does better when I'm working directly with her in a small group or even when I'm teaching the entire class—if I remember to call on her often enough.
>
> **Interventionist:** So, off task is a problem in independent work, but not when you are around. How is the quality of Charlene's work?
>
> **Teacher:** She gets it done if I keep her in from recess to do it. She does good work and seems capable, but she wastes so much time that she needs the extra time at recess. I don't mind giving up my break once in awhile, but it is getting to be an everyday occurrence.
>
> **Parent:** I think that's one of the reasons Charlene doesn't like school right now. She really enjoys the time with the kids on recess.
>
> **Interventionist:** We need to come up with a different solution. Troy, is Charlene disruptive when she's at her desk?
>
> **Teacher:** During work times she hums, sings, and talks to the other kids. I have her desk moved away from the other students, but it hasn't done much good because she gets up and bothers them.

> **Interventionist:** How does she do in other settings—in the hallways, on the playground, during music?
>
> **Teacher:** In P.E. she does just fine. Once in awhile, she's been a little loud in the hallways, but nothing out of line. The problem is really in the classroom.
>
> **Interventionist:** Let's explore how she does during different activities....

Figure 4-5 shows the interventionist's notes for Step 1.

**Figure 4-5**

---

## 25 Minute Intervention Planning Process

Student Name: Charlene Metzger    Age: 8    Grade: 3    Date: 11/18
Interventionist Name: Maria Trent    Teacher(s) Name(s): Troy Winfrey

Other Participants: Connie Metzger, mother

Starting Time: 3:15

### Step 1: Background (6 Minutes)                Stop: 3:21

- Describe the presenting problem. Identify when, where, how often, how long, etc. the problem occurs.
  - Independent work times—wanders aimlessly, bothers other children, plays with the pencil sharpener, gets drinks, etc.
  - Needs adult approval, interrupts teacher frequently when he is working with other students
  - Doesn't get work done
  - Hums and sings
  - Off task during nonteacher directed time—both independent work and cooperative group work
- Identify student strengths.
  - Socially very appropriate, well liked by other children
  - Enjoys art
  - Likes adult attention
  - Pays attention during whole class work—if she gets teacher attention
- Identify strategies already tried.
  - Discussions-Owing time during recess to get work done
  - Moved desk away from other kids already

---

## Completing Step 2: Problem and Goal

In Step 2, participants prioritize or narrow the scope of the problem and establish a positive goal. Narrowing the scope of the problem allows the planning participants to

# Chapter 4
## The Structured 25 Minute Intervention Planning Process

develop a focused plan with the greatest probability of success. Working on too many changes at once often results in frustration for both the teacher and student. To identify the priority problem, consider:

- Which behavioral change will help the student feel successful in the shortest period of time?

    The intervention plan should initially target a change that has a high probability of student success within the least amount of time. For example, if a student has problems with peer interactions, academic difficulties, and a weight problem, weight reduction would not be the first target for intervention. Though weight reduction would be a worthy long-range goal, intervention would be slowed down due to the need for medical consultation; success might be difficult to achieve; and results would not be seen for a long period of time. The student is likely to have a better chance of success if he works first on peer interactions and/or improving his academic skills. Once the student begins to experience the sense of satisfaction that accompanies success, helping the student with other problems becomes progressively easier. Success breeds success.

- Which behavioral change will help the teacher see improvements in the shortest period of time?

    The second major consideration in identifying intervention priorities is to address the problem that interferes with the teacher's teaching, or that interferes with other students' learning. The more a problem interferes with the smooth operation of the class, the sooner the problem should be addressed. If the plan is successful, both the student and teacher should feel a sense of satisfaction and accomplishment.

Once a focus has been determined, identify a positively stated goal. Though many intervention plans are designed to help a student overcome problems, a positively stated goal allows the student to take pride in his accomplishments. "Learning to respect the property of others" is a worthwhile goal. "Learning not to be destructive" is demeaning. "Learning to be trustworthy" can help a student develop a sense of self-worth; while "learning not to steal" may simply reinforce a student's sense that he is not to be trusted.

At the conclusion of Steps 1 and 2, the intervention planning members will have identified the focus on the intervention and established a positive goal statement.

> Interventionist: *In this step we need to narrow the scope of the problems and decide what can be realistically accomplished. We don't want an intervention that overwhelms Charlene or that swamps Troy with extra work. We've already narrowed the scope by identifying that this is primarily an independent work problem. Don't you think?*
>
> Teacher: *Yes. The more we talk, the more I think that is the biggest problem area.*
>
> Interventionist: *Let me quickly review what we've got. Charlene wanders around the room, playing with things like the pencil sharpener and talking to others when she should be working. She hums and makes noises at her desk. The net result is that she doesn't get her work done. Troy, can you*

> **Interventionist:** Identify which behavior interferes the most with Charlene's success and makes it hard for you and the other students to get your work done?
>
> **Teacher:** I guess there are two major problems. She causes problems when she wanders around, and she is very off task. Actually, I guess the biggest problem is wandering around. If she wasn't wandering around, maybe she'd be more on task; and if she were on task, she'd get her work done.
>
> **Interventionist:** What about the humming and other noises she makes at her desk?
>
> **Teacher:** They don't seem to bother the other students and I don't think it would bother me if I knew she was getting her work done.
>
> **Interventionist:** If we made the focus of the intervention learning to stay in her assigned place, would that seem like a good starting place?
>
> **Teacher:** Yes, but what if she still does not get her work done?
>
> **Interventionist:** Maybe Charlene's goal could be to learn to manage her work time and space. The outcome would be getting her work done.
>
> **Teacher:** Sounds good. Connie, what do you think?
>
> **Parent:** I like that. We have the same problem at home when she does homework. She is all over the place and doesn't get it done.
>
> **Interventionist:** Good. Time to move on. We were a few seconds long there. So, we'll try to make it up in the next step.

Figure 4-6 shows the interventionist's notes for Step 2.

**Figure 4-6**

---
**Step 2: Problem and Goal (2 Minutes)**          Stop __3:23__
- Narrow the scope of the problem and identify a goal.

Goal: to learn how to manage her work space and time during independent work times.

---

# Completing Step 3: Responsible Behavior and Irresponsible Behavior

In Step 3, participants identify responsible behavior that should be encouraged and irresponsible behavior that must be reduced or eliminated. Responsible behavior includes behavior that is currently in the student's repertoire as well as behavior that must be learned. When the student engages in responsible behavior, she will be demonstrating successful goal behavior.

For example, if a student is working on improving interactions with adults, responsible behavior might include saying hello in the morning, using a respectful tone of voice, nodding when the teacher addresses the student, and answering patiently if the teacher asks a question. If a student is working on managing her own in-class work, responsible behavior might include listening to directions, writing down the assignment, getting started right away, sharpening pencils before class, etc. Proactive intervention plans focus on teaching students responsible behavior. This step will help adults teach students the behavior they hope to see for goal achievement.

This step also specifies inappropriate or irresponsible behavior that should be reduced or eliminated as the student works toward goal achievement. For example, if a student is working on improving interactions with adults, irresponsible behavior might include giving the teacher a dirty look, answering the teacher in a sarcastic tone, or mimicking the teacher. If a student is working on managing her own in-class work, irresponsible behavior might include daydreaming while the teacher is giving directions, not writing down the assignment, fooling around in her desk rather than getting started on the work, etc. This step will help adults identify the behavior that should not be encouraged.

> *Interventionist:* *Now we need to identify the things that we would like to see Charlene doing during independent work times and things we don't want to see her doing.*
>
> *Teacher:* *That's pretty easy. She needs to stay on task.*
>
> *Interventionist:* *Let's use some examples to make sure it's clear. If Charlene were in her seat working quietly it would be responsible.*
>
> *Teacher:* *Of course. That is exactly what I want her doing.*
>
> *Interventionist:* *Great. I'll note that. Also, walking aimlessly about the room playing with things would be irresponsible.*

In this step, the borderline between responsible and irresponsible, or acceptable and unacceptable, behavior should be defined. For some problems this is very clear and little time is required. For other problems, the borderline between desired and undesired behavior is very hard to distinguish, making it difficult to teach students the expectations of a plan, and difficult for teachers to implement a plan. During this step, as many situations as possible should be explored to ensure that everyone fully understands what is acceptable and what is unacceptable. (See also Intervention P: *Borderlines and Consequences* for additional information on defining borderlines.)

> *Interventionist:* *We know that we don't want Charlene to disturb the other kids while they are working. What if she has a question about her work?*
>
> *Teacher:* *Well, I let the kids help each other. I don't mind if Charlene asks a neighbor a question, but I don't want her asking the kids questions unnecessarily. That's going to be hard to distinguish, isn't it?*

| | |
|---:|:---|
| Interventionist: | Maybe Charlene will need a different way to get help. I'm going to make a note under proactive strategies to suggest a question card strategy. For now, Charlene may not be able to make the fine distinction between when it's okay to go talk to another student and when it isn't okay. |
| | Let's do a little talking about out-of-seat behavior. What if her pencil lead breaks? Can she get out of her seat to sharpen it? |
| Teacher: | Yes, that would be fine unless she abuses the privilege. |
| Interventionist: | Maybe we should clarify what that means. |
| Teacher: | It would be irresponsible if she does it all the time, or if she bothers other students on her way to the sharpener. Or, it would be irresponsible if she used sharpening her pencil as an excuse to get out of her seat and wander around for a long time. This is another privilege with a lot of qualifiers. |
| Interventionist: | You may be right. Especially by the time you add in other valid reasons for getting out of her seat, such as getting a drink or turning in her work or getting her materials. |
| Teacher: | Maybe for Charlene, being out of her seat at all is inappropriate, but I hate to be unfair. |
| Interventionist: | Perhaps when we look at ways to encourage appropriate behavior, we can think of ways that Charlene might earn back the privilege. We'll need a clear list of what she should be doing during independent work times and what she should not be doing. Connie, what are you thinking? |
| Parent: | Charlene's always had a hard time sitting still. I'm not sure she can. |
| Teacher: | I know Charlene can stay with a task. She does when I'm with her. But, I really don't care whether she is sitting down or not. I just want her to be on task and not bothering others. |
| Interventionist: | We once defined the borderlines for another student who had a similar problem by defining his space with masking tape. We told him he could work in that area at his desk or on the floor, either sitting or standing. It didn't matter as long as he stayed in that space. We called it his office. |
| Parent: | I could see Charlene doing that. Is it possible to do that for her? |
| Teacher: | I like that. |
| Interventionist: | Good. I'll write that down under responsible behavior. |

# Chapter 4
## The Structured 25 Minute Intervention Planning Process

Figure 4-7 shows the interventionist's notes for Step 3.

**Figure 4-7**

**Step 3: Responsible and Irresponsible Behavior (4 Minutes)**   Stop ___3:27___

- Provide examples of responsible behavior and/or student strengths to encourage.
- Provide examples of irresponsible behavior to discourage.

| Responsible Behavior | Irresponsible Behavior |
|---|---|
| -Working quietly in her seat<br>-Getting started on her work right away<br>-Continuing to work until her work is finished<br>-Reading her SSR book<br>-Working in her office space—standing on the floor or sitting on the floor or in her seat | -Walking aimlessly about the room playing with things<br>-Distracting others by talking to them<br>-Getting up to sharpen her pencil, get a drink, etc.<br>-Out of seat talking to other students |

The examples of responsible and irresponsible behavior generated in Step 3 provide the adults with a clear and consistent definition of what constitutes appropriate and inappropriate behavior. This will help the teacher implement the plan consistently, and also provide a guide for teaching the student the specific expectations of the plan.

## Completing Step 4: Consequences

Determine whether irresponsible or inappropriate behavior will be corrected with information, be ignored, or whether a consequence will be implemented:

- Use gentle verbal reprimands when a student doesn't know that a behavior is unacceptable or is unaware of when she engages in an inappropriate behavior.

  "Sheila, you are daydreaming. Please return to you work."

- Use ignoring when the student engages in irresponsible behavior to gain attention.

  The teacher and other students carry on as though the behavior did not occur.

- Use mild consequences when the student needs to break a bad habit, or needs to know that there are consistent consequences for irresponsible behavior.

  Mild consequences include time-out, time owed, parental contacts, delaying a response, filling out a "Behavior Improvement Form," or telling the teacher what he will do differently. (For more information on consequences, see Intervention P: *Borderlines and Consequences*.)

Consequences tend to be weak interventions for reducing chronic to severe misbehavior; though they can be effective when used in combination with the more proactive strategies of this plan. If consequences are part of this plan, consider the following guidelines:

- Consequences should never humiliate the student. Humiliation may effectively eliminate an irresponsible behavior; however, the resulting emotional harm and resentment clearly outweigh any benefit. All students must be treated with dignity and respect.

- Consequences should be natural or logical results of the misbehavior. The student should understand that certain actions lead to certain consequences. The consequence should help the student make more responsible choices in the future.

- Consequences should be implemented without anger. When consequences are implemented emotionally, a student does not have to accept responsibility for his behavior. The consequence now belongs to the teacher. "I got in trouble because the teacher was mad."

- Consequences should never be imposed if the student does not know how to engage in the appropriate behavior. (See Intervention J: *Teaching Desired Behaviors*.)

Effective intervention plans focus on proactive strategies. Consequences may "make" a student behave; however consequences do not encourage students to become responsible for their own behavior. Because intervention plans are designed to teach students to be more responsible, only two minutes is given to this step. The interventionist should conduct a quick brainstorming of possibilities and then have the referring teacher select consequences that can be implemented consistently.

| | |
|---|---|
| Interventionist: | We have two minutes to decide the consequence that will be implemented whenever Charlene engages in the irresponsible behaviors we've listed. We aren't going to spend a lot of time here because we want to focus more on helping Charlene learn to work independently. Let's brainstorm some possibilities. I'll suggest a couple ideas. You could ignore Charlene's inappropriate behavior. You could use gentle reminders. You could have Charlene go to time-out. |
| Teacher: | I could have her owe one minute off her recess. |
| Interventionist: | How about a point system? If she exhibits an irresponsible behavior she wouldn't earn a point for that time period. |
| Teacher: | I could keep her after school. |
| Interventionist: | You could send her to time-out in my room. Okay. From that list, what do you think would be the best option? |
| Teacher: | I don't really think keeping her in from recess has worked, and if I ignore her that might be unfair to the rest of the kids. |
| Interventionist: | Actually, we could teach the other students to ignore Charlene's inappropriate behavior too. They need to get their work done. What do you think? |
| Teacher: | You know, Charlene really does like attention—withholding attention might be the best thing. I'd need some help teaching the other kids how to ignore. |
| Interventionist: | I can do that. Connie, we won't be teaching the kids to ignore Charlene, but we will teach them to ignore her off task behavior during independent work times. |

| | |
|---|---|
| Parent: | *I understand. Will Charlene?* |
| Interventionist: | *We can explain very carefully. Let's move on to Step 5.* |

Figure 4-8 shows the interventionist's notes for Step 4.

**Figure 4-8**

---

**Step 4:** Consequences (2 Minutes)                    Stop ___3:29___
- Determine whether irresponsible or inappropriate behavior will be corrected, ignored, or whether a consequence will be implemented.

Ignore out-of-seat and off task behavior. (Other students will need to be taught.)

---

# Completing Step 5: Proactive Strategies

Proactive strategies are the strength of any intervention plan. Proactive strategies encourage the student to engage in responsible behavior. Suggestions in this step may range from changing seats to diagnosing whether the student can do the work. Brainstorming may also include any of the sixteen interventions included in the booklets—self-control training, self-monitoring, goal setting, etc. This step should be free-flowing and encompass anything that might potentially support the student in her efforts to achieve the goal.

| | |
|---|---|
| Interventionist: | *Now we need to brainstorm any proactive strategies that might help Charlene. We've already talked about setting up a masking tape "office" to define limits but also to give Charlene a little freedom of movement. Feel free to suggest anything. This is brainstorming so we won't evaluate, just get as many ideas down as possible. Any other ideas?* |
| Teacher: | *What about doing some goal setting?* |
| Interventionist: | *I'll write that down. I also wrote down a question card strategy. That's where we give Charlene a bright colored card. If she has a question, she puts the card up on her desk. While she waits, she continues on with her work.* |
| Teacher: | *I like that. We might consider putting Charlene on a point system. I could give her a point for each half hour that she works in her office.* |
| Interventionist: | *You could have her self-monitor. At the end of each half hour, you could ask her to evaluate her office work. We could set up a little record sheet for her. Or you could give her a special job when you notice her meeting the expectations.* |
| Teacher: | *She is very good at art; I could let her help me with a bulletin board.* |

> Interventionist: Yes. It could be a reward.
>
> Teacher: Or it could just be used as a way of communicating to Charlene that she is an important member of the class. I can see from this discussion that maybe Charlene just needs attention.
>
> Interventionist: Let me also put down working on increasing positive interactions with adults. That means making sure that she gets three or four positive interactions to every correction.
>
> Teacher: We could ask the playground assistants and the other staff members to give Charlene lots of attention whenever they see her. If she got lots of attention when she was being responsible, she wouldn't have to misbehave to be noticed.
>
> Connie: I would be happy to do anything you wanted me to do at home, as long as it wasn't a punishment.
>
> Teacher: That would be great. Maybe we could set up a home reading time. Charlene reads beautifully.
>
> Interventionist: This is good. Our time is up, but there are a lot of good ideas here.

Figure 4-9 shows the interventionist's notes for Step 5.

**Figure 4-9**

---

**Step 5**: Proactive Strategies (4 Minutes)       Stop ___3:36___

- Brainstorm strategies to encourage responsible behavior. (Brainstorm, don't evaluate.)

1. Question card
2. Masking tape office
3. Goal setting
4. Self-monitoring
5. Point system'

6. Help with bulletin board
7. Increasing positive interactions with adults
8. Positive interactions with playground assistants
9. Reading at home with mom

---

# Completing Step 6: The Proactive Plan

In this step, a manageable set of strategies is selected for actual implementation. In most cases the classroom teacher will carry out the plan; therefore, the interventionist will primarily offer clarification of procedures as needed and help the teacher develop a plan that participants can realistically implement.

> Interventionist: Let's look at what we have and then decide on strategies to implement.
>
> Teacher: These are all such great ideas. I'd like to do them all.

# Chapter 4
## The Structured 25 Minute Intervention Planning Process

| | |
|---:|:---|
| Interventionist: | It would be easy to take on too much. |
| Teacher: | That's true, but a lot of these suggestions seem pretty easy. Connie, I'd like your input too. I like the masking tape office. What do you think? |
| Parent: | Yes. I think Charlene would like that. Maria, when we are through, could you help me work out something for Charlene's homework? |
| Interventionist: | Of course. Let's finish looking at the list and finalize the school plan. Then you and I can work on a homework plan. |
| Teacher: | Connie, I'm really glad you came in. I think we can help make this a better year for Charlene. Let's see. We've got the masking tape office. I'd rather not get into a point system. |
| Interventionist: | Let's eliminate all the things you don't want to do and maybe one or two of the more time-consuming strategies. Most of this will require time up front, but then will become fairly routine. |
| Teacher: | Okay. How about crossing off goal setting for now. But what do you think about a self-monitoring system? |
| Interventionist: | We could set up an assignment sheet for her to monitor her "office" work and work completion. I have a booklet on self-monitoring that will help us. |
| Teacher: | We can also work on positive interactions. Connie, would you have five or ten minutes to read with Charlene before bedtime? |
| Connie: | Yes, she still asks me to read, so I know she would like that. |
| Teacher: | Oh, and I'd like to do the question card strategy. That wouldn't be hard to do. |

Figure 4-10 shows the interventionist's notes for Step 6.

**Figure 4-10**

---
**Step 6: Proactive Plan (3 Minutes)**          Stop ___3:36___
- Select a manageable set of proactive strategies to implement.

Question card                Increasing positive interactions with adults
Masking tape office          Reading at home with mom
Self-monitoring

---

*NOTE: The interventionist should keep a completed copy of the "25 Minute Intervention Planning Process" form so that all the suggestions—whether used in the final plan or not—will be available for future use.*

# Completing Step 7: Final Details

In this step, the final details are laid out so that the plan can be implemented successfully. This includes deciding how to evaluate the effectiveness of the intervention, identifying ways other adults can assist, and summarizing each person's responsibilities.

Identify at least two ways to determine if the plan is working.

a. **Evaluation:** Identify at least two ways to determine if the plan is working.

Select two easy-to-implement procedures that will provide clear indications of whether the intervention is helping the student. Having two separate evaluation procedures tends to validate the results. One procedure can be as simple as the teacher's perceptions. Other procedures might include counting a behavior, self-monitoring forms, the student's perceptions, a series of observations from the interventionist, discipline referrals, truancy records, or the teacher's grade book, records, and rating forms.

> **Interventionist:** *In this step we need to identify a couple of ways to determine whether the plan is working. Let me suggest some ideas. One possibility would be to monitor the time Charlene spends out of her office. You could start a stop watch when she leaves her office, and then stop it when she returns to her space. The next time she leaves, you start the watch again. At the end of the day you would have the total number of minutes that she spent out of her office. We could make up a simple chart to record each day, and then we could easily see if she is getting better, worse, or staying the same. Another evaluation procedure would be to see how you are feeling about things. Is it working? Is it feasible to maintain, or is it wearing down your patience? We could just talk about this once a week. A third possibility would be to monitor her work completion, and a fourth would be to monitor Charlene's self-monitoring system.*
>
> **Teacher:** *I doubt I'd remember to start and stop a stop watch, so I'd prefer not to do that one. But, Charlene will have the self-monitoring system, and of course I will be monitoring work completion. I think I'd also like to debrief with you in a week.*
>
> **Interventionist** *Good. That's all we need.*

# Chapter 4
*The Structured 25 Minute Intervention Planning Process*   59

Figure 4-11 shows the interventionist's notes for Step 7, part a.

**Figure 4-11**

---
**Step 7:** Final Details (4 Minutes)     Stop __3:40__

a. **Evaluation:**
- Identify at least two ways to determine if the plan is working.
1. Charlene's self-monitoring system
2. Work completion
3. Weekly check-ins with Maria
---

b. **Support:** Identify things other adults can do to assist the student and teacher. (Be specific—who, what, where, when.)

This step is included to encourage collegial support and to provide the student with as much adult support as possible. Following are some types of suggestions that might be made:

- Having the student read to younger students in another classroom.
- Providing a quiet place for the student to work.
- Offering to check in with the referring staff member before a planning group meets again.
- Sharing a point chart made for another student.
- Offering to help with a parent conference.
- Offering to help with a student conference.
- Offering to cover a class while the teacher conferences with the student.
- Offering to use the student as an assistant.

For each suggestion made, the referring teacher should indicate whether it would be helpful. If so, it can be included as part of the plan.

| | |
|---|---|
| Interventionist: | *If you'd like, I can review the self-monitoring booklet and propose a system.* |
| Teacher: | *That would be great.* |
| Interventionist: | *Maybe Connie and I could come up with an assignment sheet to use for homework as well. I'll also make it a point to notice Charlene, and I can ask the playground assistants, office staff, and some of the other primary teachers to do the same. That won't be hard. She's so likable.* |

*Procedural Manual*

Figure 4-12 shows the interventionist's notes for Step 7, part b.

**Figure 4-12**

> **Step 7:** Final Details (4 Minutes)  Stop ___3:40___
> **b. Support:**
> - Identify things other adults can do to assist the student and teacher. (Be specific—who, what, where, when.)
>
> Maria—set up assignment sheet, self-monitoring with Connie today, ask other staff members to greet Charlene, chat, etc.

c. **Plan Summary:**

- Identify each person's responsibilities and when actions will be taken;
- Identify who will discuss the plan with the student and when; and
- Schedule follow-up.

Participants in planning meetings often get carried away as they develop proactive plans for students. Enthusiasm runs high, only to find that within a few days nothing has happened. Implementation is the hard step, so it is imperative that everyone is clear about their duties and responsibilities for implementing the plan.

| | |
|---|---|
| Interventionist: | I think we have a wonderful plan. We have three minutes left to wrap it up, so I want to be sure we are all very clear about what we will be doing and when. Charlene's goal will be to learn to manage her work space and time. To help her reach her goal, I'll need to teach the other students how to ignore Charlene's behavior when she is off task. Troy, would Tuesday at 9:00 work? |
| Teacher: | Yes. |
| Parent: | Is Charlene going to feel okay about this? |
| Interventionist: | We will need to discuss it with Charlene ahead of time. She is a bright girl and we can explain that we all have things to work on. We will let the other kids know we are doing this because Charlene is part of our classroom family. Then we need to be extra supportive of Charlene. |
| Parent: | I can see how this will help her. I guess I just get worried. |
| Teacher: | I understand. I'll do all I can to help everyone understand that this is part of our class effort to support and help each other. |
| Interventionist: | Good. Let's set a date to talk this through with Charlene. Troy, how would it be if you, Charlene, and I met for lunch on Monday? That way I can fill you both in on the self-monitoring system. We need to watch your lunch time though. |

# Chapter 4
*The Structured 25 Minute Intervention Planning Process*

**Teacher:** That's okay. I eat with kids on special occasions all through the year. Charlene and I can set up her office when we're through.

**Interventionist:** Sounds great!

**Teacher:** I think it will be fun. I'll figure out another special time to spend with her, maybe the following Monday. That would get two weeks off to a nice start.

**Interventionist:** Good. Let's return a minute to the office set-up. Troy, can you show Charlene all the ways she could work appropriately within her office and teach her to use the question card? Maybe do some role playing—you pretend to be her and Charlene can let you know when you are working hard. You can also role play how to use the self-monitoring system we come up with.

**Teacher:** Yes, we can do some role playing after lunch on Monday.

**Interventionist:** Good. Connie, you and I will work out the self-monitoring system after Troy leaves. Troy, I will make it a point to check in with you about this at staff meetings. I'll keep records so we can watch how things are going. Let's see, we also want to focus on positive interactions when Charlene is working appropriately in her office. Troy, that means trying to be conscious of when she is being responsible for herself.

**Teacher:** I may have to tie a string around my finger, but I'll make it a point to watch out for Charlene.

**Interventionist:** One way is to keep ten popsicle sticks in a box—every time you interact positively with Charlene, take one stick out. The box is your reminder. Or, just make it a point to notice Charlene between every transition. When you finish a student conference, you can monitor her. When you finish working with a small group, you can monitor.

**Teacher:** I actually think the popsicle stick thing might work. Let me think that one over. You know, we didn't decide what to do if Charlene doesn't get her work done. I don't like keeping her in for recess.

**Interventionist:** Let's try this for two weeks and see if work completion increases without consequences. We can tell Charlene during the conference that we want to help her monitor her own work, and let her enjoy the time at recess with her friends.

**Teacher:** I like that. It gives her some nice confidence building to begin with.

**Interventionist:** Good. I think that does it. Oops, Connie you also wanted to do home reading. (Connie nods.) Now, one last detail. When shall we have our first follow-up conference?

Schedule a time for a follow-up meeting before ending the planning session. If possible, the interventionist should check in with the referring teacher within a day or two of implementation. During the implementation phase, plans frequently need adjustment and fine tuning. Occasionally, teachers need assistance implementing unfamiliar procedures. Once the plan is running smoothly, follow-up can be scheduled less frequently.

> **Interventionist:** *Troy and Connie, do you have time to arrange a follow-up? I'd like to set a date for two weeks. We can always cancel if the time isn't needed.*
>
> **Parent:** *I'd like that.*
>
> **Interventionist** *How about a follow-up meeting for Dec. 9 at 3:00. Is that okay? (Connie and Troy both give their assent.) I'm very pleased with this plan. There is a lot to it, but it's supportive and once it's set up it'll be manageable. I'll summarize everything in writing and get you each a copy within the next day or two.*

Figure 4-13 shows the interventionist's notes for Step 7, part c.

**Figure 4-13**

---

### Step 7: Final Details (4 Minutes)          Stop __3:40__

**c. Plan Summary:**

- Identify each person's responsibilities and when actions will be taken;
- Identify who will discuss the plan with the student and when; and
- Schedule follow-up.

| Who | Responsibilities | Date(s) |
|---|---|---|
| Maria | Teach kids to ignore | Tuesday, Nov. 21, 9:00 A.M. |
| Troy, Charlene | Set up office | Monday, Nov. 20, after lunch |
| Troy | Teach Charlene how to work in office and use question card | Monday, Nov. 20, after lunch |
| Troy | Meet with Charlene | Monday, Nov. 27 |
| Maria, Connie | Self-monitoring system | Today |
| Troy, Maria | Staff meeting check-ins | Each Wednesday |
| Troy | Positive interactions | Approx. ten times each day |
| Maria and other staff | Positive interactions | Each day |
| Connie | Bedtime reading | Every week night |

Discussion With the Student:
Who __Troy and Maria__          Date __Monday, Nov. 20__    Time __12:00 P.M.__

Follow-Up Meeting:
Who __Troy, Maria, and Connie__     Date __Dec. 9__     Time __3:00 P.M.__

## Completing the Plan

To complete the process, the interventionist should give each participant a summary of the plan (see Figure 4-14) outlining all responsibilities and timelines in writing. Good intentions and the best laid plans can easily become lost in the normal demands of daily activities.

**Figure 4-14**

### Intervention Summary Form

Student: Charlene Metzger     Date: 11/19

Teacher(s): Troy Winfrey

Other Participants: Connie Metzger (mother), Maria Trent (interventionist)

**Goal:**
To learn how to manage her work space and time during independent work

**Student Responsibilities:** Charlene

- Set up office
- Work on "office behavior"
- Write down assignments, start times, and finish times on self-monitoring form (assignment sheet)
- Rate work effort (− ✓ +)
- Stay in office during work times

**Teacher Responsibilities:** Troy

- Monday, Nov. 20 lunch: describe the goal to Charlene, office plan, and ignoring
  - Help Charlene set up her office and teach her how to work appropriately within her space (including question card) by role playing
- Monday, Nov. 27: Meet with Charlene
- Wednesdays:
  Check in with Maria, during staff meetings (have work completion information ready and Charlene's self-monitoring records)
- All times:
  - Work on interacting with Charlene when she is being responsible
  - Help Charlene with her self-monitoring form
  - Congratulate Charlene when assignments are checked off

**Interventionist Responsibilities:** Maria

- Select or develop a self-monitoring form for Charlene with Connie (done—see attached)
- Monday, Nov. 20 lunch: teach Charlene and Troy how self-monitoring system works; find out if Charlene wants to do something with Troy during class ignoring lesson
- Tuesday, Nov. 21, 9:00 A.M.: Teach Charlene's class to ignore her inappropriate behavior
- Ask other staff members to interact positively with Charlene (done)

**Parent/Guardian Responsibilities:** Connie

- Read at bedtime with Charlene—just a nice, positive time
- Set up home office and have Charlene use an assignment sheet for self-monitoring

**Follow-Up:**

See you Dec. 9 at 3:00 for a ten-minute follow-up meeting.

*NOTE: A copy of this form is provided in the "Reproducible Materials" at the end of this manual.*

# Providing Follow-up

The first follow-up consists of a quick, informal check-in on the first or second day of implementation. This brief check-in allows the teacher and interventionist to make any immediate modifications that might be needed. A follow-up conference should then be scheduled for about a week later, and additional follow-up conferences would be planned during the first conference.

During the follow-up conferences, participants evaluate student progress and make modifications to the plan if needed:

- Redesign the intervention if the student is making no progress or getting worse.

  If the student shows no progress, the plan may need to be redesigned. However, prior to abandoning a plan, there should be two independent means of verifying that the plan is not working. If a student has been making good progress, but "blows it" one day, a teacher may feel that the student hasn't made any progress at all. Evaluation information and the support of the interventionist can help the teacher and student stay on course.

- Modify the intervention to provide more support and structure if student progress is very slow or has come to a halt.

  Because intervention planning involves trial and error, it may become apparent that the student needs more assistance.

- Maintain the intervention if the student is making good progress.

  If the student is making steady progress toward a goal, the plan should be maintained until the student demonstrates continuous success in achieving the goal.

- Fade the intervention if there is a high probability that the student can maintain success.

  Fading is accomplished by gradually providing less structure and support. Some interventions are automatically faded as the student becomes successful.

| | |
|---|---|
| Interventionist: | *I'm anxious to see how Charlene is doing.* |
| Teacher: | *I brought her self-monitoring chart and also my record of work completion.* |
| Interventionist | *How are things going?* |
| Teacher: | *I think that things are going really well. Charlene has done a nice job of completing her self-monitoring chart. She is very, very honest in her self-assessment. A few times I even thought she was a little hard on herself. As you can see, she does better in the morning than in the afternoon (see Figure 4-15).* |

# Chapter 4
## The Structured 25 Minute Intervention Planning Process

**Figure 4-15**

```
Charlene's Work Log

Date  11/28

Assignment              A.M., P.M., or      Work Finished    Effort Evaluation
                        Homework
Reading                 A.M.                yes              -  ⓥ   +
Journal                 A.M.                yes              -  ✓   ⊕
Math                    A.M.                yes              -  ✓   ⊕
Social Studies          P.M.                no               ⊖  ✓   +
Math                    Homework            yes              -  ⓥ   +
                                                             -  ✓   +

Key:  -  got distracted and didn't finish work
      ✓  got distracted, but got to work
      +  kept working from start to finish
```

Interventionist: *How is her work completion overall?*

Teacher: *Given that she hardly got anything in at all before this, I would say that she has come a long way. She got all of her morning work in for the week. Afternoon is still a problem—depending on what we're doing.*

Interventionist: *Should we adjust the plan a bit for the afternoon?*

Teacher: *Let's wait one more week. This has been quite an adjustment. Let me just talk with Charlene.*

Interventionist: *I think that's a good idea. You could even do a little goal setting.*

Teacher: *That's a good idea. Do you have forms I could look at?*

Interventionist: *Sure. I'll loan you my goal setting booklet. Let me know if you'd like assistance.*

Teacher: *I will. I'm pleased with Charlene's progress and would like to keep working on this.*

Follow-up not only provides an opportunity to evaluate student progress and to make modifications as needed, but it also provides all participants in the plan with continued support. Intervention is often successful if a focus on goals can be maintained, and is often only temporarily successful if abruptly forgotten. Even after the intervention has been faded, the interventionist should periodically check to see that all is continuing on course.

Interventionist: *It's been a week since we took Charlene completely off the self-monitoring chart. How's it going?*

Teacher: *Pretty good. I think she kind of misses the chart though.*

> Interventionist: You know, there isn't anything wrong with her keeping it.
>
> Teacher: Maybe I'll tell her it's optional, that she can use it if she wants. I have another student on the system now and I think Charlene may be a little jealous.
>
> Interventionist: I think it would be a great idea for Charlene to have the option of using her self-monitoring chart. I'd also like to take her for an ice cream cone as a reward for all of her progress. Do you think I could take her to the cafeteria for about ten minutes this afternoon?
>
> Teacher: I'm sure she'd love that.
>
> Interventionist: I just want to remind Charlene how proud we are of her. Is she still using the masking tape office?
>
> Teacher: Oh, yes. I think that she still needs that little prompt, but I've told her that since she's kind of her own manager now that she can leave her office to get one drink of water in the morning.
>
> (See the booklets Intervention I: *Goal Setting and Contracting*, Intervention K: *Self-Monitoring*, Intervention L: *Structured Reinforcement Systems*, Intervention O: *Increasing Positive Interactions*, and Intervention P: *Borderlines and Consequences* for more information on the strategies referenced in this scenario.)

# Conclusion

When a problem is mild to moderate, a structured agenda with time limits can result in an effective intervention plan. Though the time limits restrict an in-depth exploration of the problem, they do allow busy professionals to develop reasonably sound interventions. School staff cannot spend hours developing plans for every student with problems. The 25 minute process provides the option of developing plans before a student is in crisis and requires in-depth planning.

# CHAPTER 5

## The In-Depth Intervention Decision Guide (IDG) Process

THE INTERVENTION DECISION Guide (IDG) process is the most detailed planning format discussed in this program (see Figure 5-1). The IDG process is recommended when a problem is moderate to severe, and complex enough to require detailed and systematic planning. Collaborative groups may wish to begin planning with the "IDG" form, or use this process if informal collaboration or the 25 minute planning process have not resulted in improvements.

**Figure 5-1: The Intervention Process**

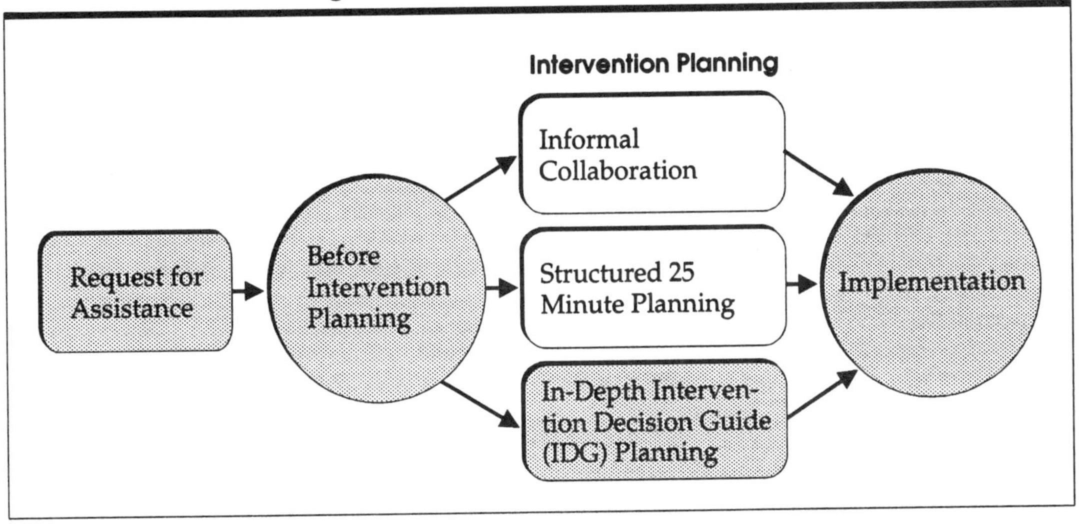

*Intervention Planning*

Request for Assistance → Before Intervention Planning → Informal Collaboration / Structured 25 Minute Planning / In-Depth Intervention Decision Guide (IDG) Planning → Implementation

The "Intervention Decision Guide" form ("IDG") involves a four-stage process to develop intervention plans for at-risk students. The four stages of the process are: Background, Preparation (for intervention planning), Intervention Design, and Implementation. Figure 5-2 shows the four-page layout of the "IDG." (Larger illustrations of all the sections of this form will be provided throughout this chapter.)

# Chapter 5
## The In-Depth Intervention Decision Guide (IDG) Process

**Figure 5-2 The "IDG"**

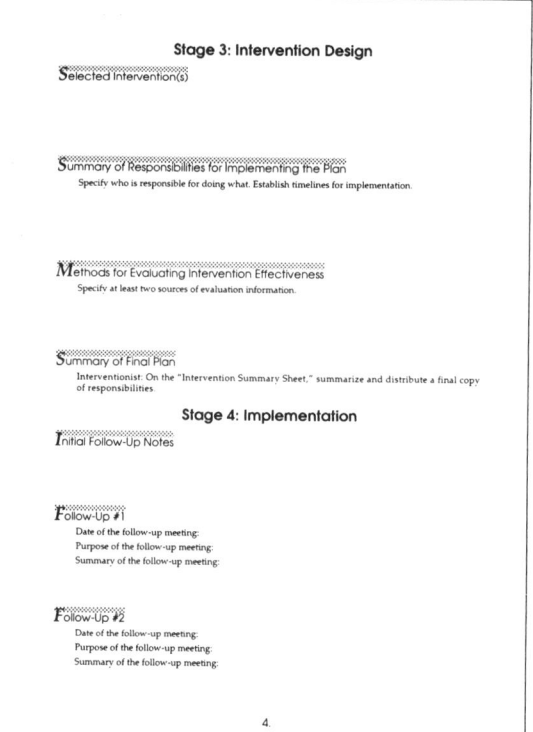

NOTE: A copy of this form is provided in the "Reproducible Materials" at the end of this manual.

# Completing Preliminary Steps

Before intervention planning begins, the interventionist and referring teacher complete preliminary steps, as outlined in Chapter 2.

| | |
|---|---|
| Interventionist: | Marge, I got your note about Travis. Do you have five minutes to talk? |
| Teacher: | Sure. I knew that Travis might be a handful, but was hoping we could work things out. Unfortunately, his behavior is deteriorating. |
| Interventionist: | I'm glad you got in touch. I suspect we'll want to do some long-range planning, but for now can you summarize the major problem? |
| Teacher: | He's accelerating the attention-getting stuff. He's obnoxious—socially inappropriate with the other kids. |
| Interventionist: | Does he do anything that's dangerous to anyone? |
| Teacher: | You mean fighting or anything? No. He's just a pest, always doing things to be noticed. |
| Interventionist: | Have you talked with Travis' mom? |
| Teacher: | I suppose she doesn't know what's happening. I called early in the year to let her know I was glad to have Travis in class. I was hoping that if we got off to a positive start things would be okay. Wrong! |
| Interventionist: | What does Travis say? |
| Teacher: | I've had him stay in at recess because it's the only time we can talk. He says stuff like, "Mom says I'm a rotten kid." |
| Interventionist: | Would you mind if I scheduled an observation? Then I'd like to help you develop an intervention plan. |
| Teacher: | Good. I was hoping that a lot of positive interactions would work, but it isn't enough. |
| Interventionist: | I've worked with Travis' family before. His mother is hard to reach because she works two jobs. I'd like to get her involved, but she may not be able to come in. However, we'll need her permission. Do you want to call her? |
| Teacher: | Yes. I'll try this evening. I'm feeling kind of guilty about not having talked with her sooner. |
| Interventionist: | We have a Teacher Assistance Team meeting scheduled for next week, but the docket is full and I think we may need to do more in-depth planning for Travis immediately. |

> Teacher: I agree.
>
> Interventionist: Let's meet during your music class. Should we see if Arnie (the principal) can sit in? Travis used to spend a lot of time in the office. But you know how Arnie is; they have a pretty good relationship.
>
> Teacher: I haven't sent Travis to the office because I like to work things out in the classroom, but you're right. Arnie would be very helpful.
>
> Interventionist: I'll also invite Kara to the meeting. Travis gave her a rough time last year, but they ended the year very positively. She may be able to give us some insight.
>
> Teacher: Do you think we can get someone to cover her class?
>
> Interventionist: I'll see. If not, I'll talk with her beforehand.

Once the meeting is scheduled, the interventionist fills out the top of the "IDG" form as shown in Figure 5-3.

**Figure 5-3**

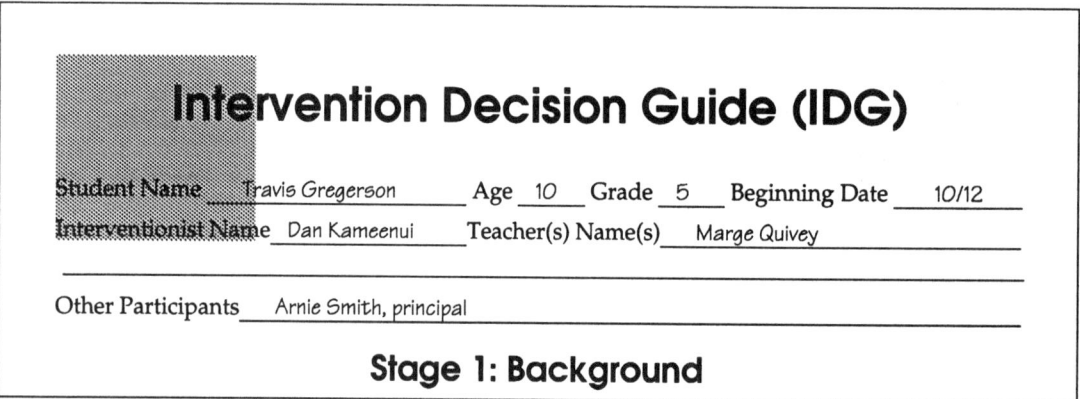

# Beginning the Planning Meeting

The interventionist (or referring teacher) should convene the meeting by welcoming each participant and establishing an atmosphere of support and advocacy for the student. One person should be designated as the recorder and the notes taken should be saved for later reference. (Usually, the recorder is the interventionist.)

# Completing Stage 1: Background

In Stage 1, the interventionist and other intervention planning participants gather background information that might be relevant to the problem. Because the "IDG" provides structure but no time limits, the interventionist must skillfully guide the process—not spending so much time that the meeting drags on, but enough to obtain the needed information. The more information that the participants have, the greater the likelihood that they can develop an intervention plan that is responsive to the needs of the student.

## Reason for the Referral and Description of the Problem(s)

Once a positive atmosphere has been established, the interventionist begins the process by noting the nature of the referral (e.g., the student's classroom teacher has requested assistance, the student has academic difficulties or failing grades, the student has had a certain number of office referrals, or the student's parents have requested assistance).

Generally, the referring teacher summarizes the problem and elaborates on the types of behavior that interfere with student success.

> Interventionist: *Marge, go ahead and describe the problems you are having with Travis.*
>
> Teacher: *Travis seems to be the kind of kid who needs attention—constantly. He blurts out comments in class and calls the other kids names. I don't think it's really malicious. He just wants attention and goes about getting it in all the wrong ways.*
>
> Within a few minutes the interventionist has taken notes as shown in Figure 5-4.

**Figure 5-4**

---

### Stage 1: Background

**R**eason for the Referral and Description of the Problem(s)

Ms. Quivey has requested assistance.
Travis has problems with excessive "attention-seeking" behavior:
 -Blurts out comments in class.
 -Calls other students names.
 -Always has something to say, tattles, asks unnecessary questions, comments on everything.
 -Teases other students inappropriately, harasses them by pushing their things off desks. He often pokes others, pushes, yanks on hair, grabs . . . .

---

## Code Red (Is it an emergency situation?)

Following the "IDG" form, the participants next identify whether the problem presents a crisis.

## The behavior is a threat to physical safety.

If the behavior is a threat to anyone's physical safety, the planning participants should proceed immediately to Intervention A: *Managing Physically Dangerous Behavior*. This Intervention discusses physical safety issues, contacting parents/guardians, record-keeping, considering special education referral, and teaching students to manage their own behavior. (If preliminary steps have been taken prior to intervention planning, the question of physical safety may have already been addressed.) Once *Managing Physically Dangerous Behavior* has been implemented, the participants can return to the "IDG" to address the causes of the problem and establish a long-range plan.

## The behavior is so disruptive the teacher can't teach.

If the behavior is so severe that the teacher cannot be expected to teach while it is occurring, the planning participants should proceed immediately to Intervention B: *Managing Severely Disruptive Behavior*. This intervention assists a teacher in developing an immediate plan for dealing with highly disruptive behavior. With this intervention, the student's parent(s) (or guardian) are contacted and temporary procedures are designed to focus on appropriate behavior while providing consistent consequences for minor to severe misbehavior. Once these temporary procedures have been set up, the planning participants can return to the "IDG" for more in-depth planning.

Whether the behavior is "severely disruptive" or just a "major annoyance" is a judgment call depending largely on the classroom teacher's skills and tolerance levels. Because *Managing Severely Disruptive Behavior* may include the student's removal from the classroom, independent confirmation of the student's disruptive behavior is recommended. The nature of the confirmation may be direct observation by the interventionist or administrator, the fact that parents of other students have complained, or reports of disruptive behavior in other settings.

| | |
|---|---|
| Interventionist: | *Marge, you mentioned earlier that Travis wasn't exhibiting any physically dangerous behavior, and there is no history of anything that would cause us to be alarmed.* |
| Teacher: | *Right. I also don't see the behavior as being so disruptive that I can't teach.* |
| Principal: | *I'm glad to hear that. Travis was so disruptive last year that he was removed from the classroom several times. I should stop by and let him know that I've noticed his progress this year.* |
| Teacher: | *It's also good for me to know that Travis has made improvements. I'm sure he would love to see you.* |

## Notes on the Problem(s)   What, Where, When, Why

This is the appropriate place on the form to comprehensively summarize the problem behavior. What does the student do? Where do the problems occur? How often do the problems occur and how often do they last? The information may come from the student's classroom teacher, but efforts should be made to include input from observations and from anyone else who may have contact with the student—playground assistants, the principal, the counselor, and so on. (The interventionist may need to interview staff members who are not a part of the intervention planning group.)

### Are there situations that seem to set off the problem behavior?

Situations that seem to trigger the problem behavior should be identified. If a student fights with peers, what sort of interactions tend to precipitate a fight? If a student is overtly defiant of teacher authority, what events usually occur prior to insubordinate acts? When specific triggers can be identified, the intervention will focus on teaching the student to manage his or her behavior under those conditions, or to avoid situations that result in problems.

### Where do the problem(s) tend to occur?

Do problems occur only in the classroom? Does the student have difficulty in the hallways, in special settings like the library and music room, on the playground, or in the cafeteria? Do the student's parents report similar problems at home? When problems are pervasive across all settings, the behavior may be firmly ingrained in the student's repertoire. On the other hand, if the problem only occurs in one or two settings, there may be something specific about the setting(s) that results in problems.

### When do the problem(s) tend to occur?

Try to determine whether there is a pattern to the misbehavior. Do problems occur during certain times of the day? Are mornings better than afternoons? Do problems tend to occur more frequently on certain days? If a pattern is detected, it may help with intervention planning. For example, if a student has tantrums and angry outbursts more frequently on Mondays, weekends may be hard for the student. The student may be tired. Or the home situation may be particularly disruptive on weekends. The student may feel torn after custody visits. Given this situation, the interventionist can try to collaborate with the student's parents to help reduce stress on weekends as well as intensify school intervention efforts on Mondays.

### Are there situations in which the problem(s) seem less prevalent?

Noting situations in which the student's behavior tends to be better (or at least less severe) may provide insight on how to create a plan that will help the student be successful. For example, if the student does not tend to misbehave during music class, the music teacher might be able to provide information on the student's needs, or perhaps some aspect of music could be used as a tool to increase the student's motivation in other settings.

### How often do the problem(s) occur? How long does the behavior last?

Knowing the frequency and duration of problems can also be critical information in intervention planning. If a young student throws tantrums once or twice a week, the problem may not seem severe. However, if the tantrums last for 60 to 90 minutes, the student may need an intensive intervention plan. Sometimes it is useful for the teacher or interventionist to take data on the problem prior to planning an intervention or prior to implementing a plan.

## What seems to be maintaining (reinforcing) the student's misbehavior?

Try to identify what the student seems to achieve or gain through the misbehavior. If the misbehavior occurs frequently, ask, "What's in it for the student?" Does the student gain attention through the misbehavior? Does the student control situations? Does the student handle his frustration or anger by misbehaving? Is the student able to avoid doing work? Keep in mind that when a problem behavior occurs frequently, it is meeting a need of the student. For example, if a student consistently gains teacher attention for her misbehavior, the student may enjoy the adult contact—even though it is negative. If the misbehavior consistently leads to removal from the room, removal from the room is probably satisfying to the student at some level. It is not always possible to determine the specific events or situations that reinforce and perpetuate the problem; however this process may lead to useful insight that in turn will assist in intervention planning.

Interventionist: *It's nice to know that Travis hasn't slipped backwards this year. Marge, it may not feel like your efforts have paid off, but it sounds like we are making progress with Travis. We need to take some notes on when the problems seem to occur. Have you noticed any events that seem to set Travis off?*

Teacher: *No. He just seems to want attention all the time.*

Interventionist: *I didn't notice any patterns when I observed. However, he clearly wants peer attention. What about settings?*

Teacher: *His problems are mostly in the classroom, although he's had a few problems in the cafeteria and on the playground.*

Interventionist: *Do you notice any patterns in terms of time of day or day of the week?*

Teacher: *No.*

Interventionist: *What about situations in which the problems don't usually occur?*

Teacher: *The only thing I can think of off hand is that he seems to do better during highly directed activities like math than he does during more self-directed types of tasks such as art.*

Interventionist: *How often do the problems occur?*

Teacher: *He wants attention in just about every activity you could mention—small group work, large group discussions, independent work. He is better during instruction, but I give him more than his fair share of attention to keep him on track.*

Interventionist: *I think the reason for Travis' misbehavior is fairly clear—attention.*

Teacher: *Yes, but he may also be doing it for power. I can't tell.*

Principal: *I don't know about that either. He's a really sharp kid. His behavior may be a little manipulative.*

Within a few minutes the interventionist has taken notes on the problems as shown in Figure 5-5.

# Chapter 5
## The In-Depth Intervention Decision Guide (IDG) Process

**Figure 5-5**

---

**Notes on the Problem(s)    What, Where, When, Why**

(Arnie notes improvements over last year. Travis seems to be in better control.)

Are there situations that seem to set off the problem behavior?

    No specific events have been identified, just a generalized need for attention from the teacher and peers.

Where do the problem(s) tend to occur?

    Ms. Quivey is mainly concerned about the classroom although students sometimes report that Travis is a problem on the playground and in the cafeteria.

When do the problem(s) tend to occur?

    Time(s) of day:   Throughout

    Day(s) of the week:   No specific pattern is apparent.

Are there situations in which the problem(s) seem less prevalent?

    Travis seems to be more successful in teacher directed activities than in self-directed activities.

How often do the problem(s) occur? How long does the behavior last?

    The attention-seeking behavior feels fairly constant to Ms. Quivey.

What seems to be maintaining (reinforcing) the student's misbehavior? (Check as many as apply.)

    ☑ Attention    ☐ Venting frustration or anger    ☐ Other _____

    ☑ Power    ☐ Escape

**Notes:**

The main motivation seems to be Travis' need for attention from both adults and peers. Problems may also involve Travis trying to exert power and control over those around him.

---

## Strengths of the Student (at Least Three)

For this section, the participants identify at least three strengths of the student. When problems are severe and/or pervasive, it is easy to lose sight of the student's strengths and positive qualities. This step prevents an entirely negative focus during intervention planning and gives the team some potential ways to address the problems. For example, a student who is disruptive but also very funny could earn the right to do a "stand up" routine for the class by cooperating in class for a specified period of time. If a student is very athletic, a mentor might be selected who could play basketball with the student (see Intervention G: *Mentoring*). If Intervention L: *Structured Reinforcement Systems* is considered for a student, time in the gym may be a potential reinforcer. The power of intervention planning will always be enhanced by keeping a focus on student strengths.

Interventionist: *Now we need to identify Travis' strengths—things he likes and is good at.*

Teacher: *I know I tend to forget about how capable Travis is. When he's been obnoxious, I forget that he is actually one of my strongest students. Academics come easily to him.*

Principal: *You know, last year we discovered that he is quite musical. The music teacher reported that he has a strong sense of rhythm and carries a tune well.*

Teacher: *He's also very good at soccer. I don't know about other sports, but in soccer the kids all want him on their team.*

> Interventionist: *Other things? He's a talented kid, isn't he? It's too bad he doesn't recognize that. Let's move on, but we can come back to this if you think of anything else.*

Figure 5-6 shows the interventionist's notes for the student strength section.

**Figure 5-6**

---
**Strengths of the Student (at Least Three)**
1. Strong student, academically very capable
2. Musical
3. Good at soccer
---

## The Teacher(s)' Goal or Desired Outcome

The purpose of this section is to clarify what the teacher hopes to accomplish through intervention planning. Because the purpose is to clarify the teacher's goals, the interventionist should not only determine what the teacher hopes to accomplish, but also "what the teacher can't live with any longer." Student success is determined to a large extent by the teacher's perceptions. Therefore, an intervention must focus not only on improving student behavior, but also on addressing any misbehavior that the teacher cannot tolerate. Listening to the teacher's initial goals better equips the planning participants to identify major priorities.

In this section, help the teacher to be as specific as possible. For example:

> Teacher: *I want April to be more respectful.*
>
> Interventionist: *Tell me a little more. What would you like her to do when she first enters the room?*
>
> Teacher: *I want April to begin the day by putting her things in her cubby. When I greet her, I would like her to acknowledge my greeting by nodding or saying hello.*

Listen carefully to find out what the referring teacher really wants. When a teacher feels cut off, the collaborative nature of the planning may be damaged. By listening and writing down *all* the points the teacher makes, the teacher's perceptions are valued. The goal of the intervention should be a joint decision that incorporates all the participants' input. Unrealistic expectations can be tempered later.

> Interventionist: *Marge, at his point we'd like to find out what you hope to accomplish with an intervention plan.*
>
> Teacher: *Hmmm, I know what I don't want him to do.*
>
> Interventionist: *We can begin with what you would rather not live with anymore.*

# Chapter 5
## The In-Depth Intervention Decision Guide (IDG) Process

> **Teacher:** I can ignore the rude comments to me, but I don't want Travis to bother the other kids. I guess it's the physical stuff that's the worst. Even the kids have begun to learn to ignore his comments. We've talked about that a lot. But, when he grabs something, or pushes things off desks, or pokes and grabs at others... none of us can handle it.
>
> **Interventionist:** That helps narrow this down. Would you say then that the least tolerable behavior involves physically harassing others?
>
> **Teacher:** Yes, definitely.
>
> **Interventionist:** Now, what would you like to see Travis accomplish?
>
> **Teacher:** I guess I'd like to see him less desperate for attention. I'd like him to feel valued. I'd like him to be happy with all of his wonderful talents.
>
> **Interventionist:** So, you'd like to see him feel valued and to value himself.
>
> **Principal:** You know, he really has made some progress. Last year the major goal we had was for Travis to control himself. It sounds like he must be much less impulsive.

Figure 5-7 shows the interventionist's notes for the teacher goal section.

**Figure 5-7**

---
*T*he Teacher(s)' Goal or Desired Outcome
What would the teacher(s) like to have happen? What can't the teacher(s) "live with" any longer?
Can't tolerate/don't like: Agitating other kids, pushing things off desks, poking, grabbing at others
Goal: To feel valued and to value himself—need less attention
To respect other students

---

## Notes on Parental Involvement

Parental contact and involvement are necessary components of intervention planning. Parents have a right, both legally and ethically, to know when their child is having a problem and that the staff is concerned enough to initiate intervention planning. By this point, parents should have been contacted, and permission obtained for intervention planning. In some cases, parents will have been invited to take part in the intervention process to the degree that they can and wish to be involved (see Chapter 2). Whether actively involved or not, families should be brought into the process as much as possible. Their wishes should be explored, and their input valued.

In this section of the form, the recorder should include information from earlier contacts.

> **Interventionist:** I contacted Travis' mother after Marge did. We anticipated that Mrs. Gregerson would not be able to make it for this meeting. I asked her what she hoped for Travis this year and her response was that she wants him to stay out of trouble, and that she doesn't want to be bothered by the school.
>
> **Teacher:** I got a similar response. She also said that she had given up on Travis. She told me that her older kids had dropped out of school and that she didn't expect Travis to stay in school forever. She said that whatever we needed to do was okay with her—she did send the permission slip.
>
> **Principal:** I think she talks a bit of a tough line, but has secret hopes that Travis will do better. At one meeting last year, she raved about how smart he was. I think she goes up and down.
>
> **Interventionist:** Well, we have her okay to go ahead. I'd be happy to be the contact person if you'd like, Marge.
>
> **Teacher:** That would be great. I'd like her to have the sense that we aren't giving up on Travis. Maybe then she'll get her hopes back up again.

Figure 5-8 shows the interventionist's notes for the parental involvement section.

**Figure 5-8**

---
**Notes on Parental Involvement**

Contact date(s):  October 5 - Marge
October 7 - Dan

Notes on the contact(s):

Marge: Mother says to go ahead with planning—returned permission slip. Wants Travis to get along, but expects him to drop out eventually like brother and sister.
Dan: Wants Travis to stay out of trouble; doesn't want to be bothered by the school.

What would the parent(s) or guardian like to have happen?

Mother does not express expectations; however, in the past has voiced hope that Travis will be the one kid who makes it.

---

## Input From the Student

In this section, the interventionist records the student's perceptions of the problem. The teacher should have already discussed the problem with the student at a neutral time. If this hasn't yet occurred, Intervention C: *Planned Discussions* should be implemented. Whenever the student discussion occurs, it is important for the interventionist to notice and record his or her impressions about the student's responses to the following questions: Does the student seem motivated to do better? Does the student understand the problem? Does the student feel powerless to change? Student input can provide important information for selecting intervention strategies.

# Chapter 5
## The In-Depth Intervention Decision Guide (IDG) Process

> **Interventionist:** Marge, you've had several discussions with Travis at this point. Do you want to share his comments?
>
> **Teacher:** Well, he says that he knows he's a brat, but that he doesn't know why.
>
> **Principal:** When I ran into him yesterday, he said he liked Ms. Quivey, but that he was 'bad' sometimes.
>
> **Teacher:** The last time I talked to him, he said that he'd like to try to be better but that he just doesn't know what to do. He'd like the other kids to like him.

Figure 5-9 shows the interventionist's notes for the student input section.

**Figure 5-9**

> *Input From the Student*
> - Says he's a brat, that he's bad, and doesn't know how to change.
> - Seems to want to change.
> - Wants the other students to like him.

## Other Information

The more complex the problem, the more important information gathering becomes. Input from previous teachers and from other staff members who may have contact with the student (e.g., playground supervisors, counselors, etc.) should be gathered and recorded. In addition, the interventionist should examine the student's records to look for relevant information regarding medical history, academic problems, or involvement with outside agencies such as mental health or juvenile authorities, and so on.

> **Interventionist:** I talked with Kara about Travis' third grade year. Arnie, maybe you can also help us out since you worked with Travis last year.
>
> **Principal:** Yes, but we didn't go into in-depth intervention planning. We did some 25 minute sessions and Kara felt they were helpful.
>
> **Interventionist:** Kara described many of the same problems you have Marge, only she also mentioned that Travis was very impulsive and angry a lot. She said that he got really mad at her at times and threw tantrums.
>
> **Principal:** Yes, we used an office time-out for those times.

Figure 5-10 shows the interventionist's notes for the other information section.

**Figure 5-10**

> **O**ther Information
>
> Input from previous teachers:
>   Kara Hershey (grade 3) reports that Travis was occasionally impulsive and very angry. He threw tantrums and was timed-out in the office several times last year. Travis made progress with an intervention plan that included time-out, ignoring, and positive attention—such as giving special reports to the class, being line leader, etc.
>
> Input from other staff who know the student (assistants, counselor, specialists, etc.):
>   Playground aides report continued problems with other kids, also noting minor physical harassment. He is often benched. Enjoys soccer season and has fewer problems when games are organized.
>
> Review of the student's records:
>   -Strong academic test scores, well above average.
>   -Problems noted for behavior in second grade.
>   -Considered for hyperactivity in first grade; physician reported no medical problems.

## Interventions Tried and Their Results

In this final section of Stage 1, any interventions that have been tried to date, how long they were implemented, and if they were successful should be listed. When designing the intervention, the planning participants should capitalize on anything that has worked in the past and avoid interventions that have been proven to be ineffective.

> **Interventionist:** Marge, tell us what you've tried so far and then we'll also note what we know about last year's intervention efforts.
>
> **Teacher:** I've worked hard on positive interactions. I've tried to catch Travis being mature and appropriate whenever I can. When I hear about his problems last year, I realize that maybe this has helped. He hasn't thrown any tantrums this year. The more I think about it, his biggest problems really are with the other kids. He is rude occasionally in class, but it really isn't so bad that I can't ignore it. I think it's just throw-back behavior.
>
> **Interventionist:** From last year, we can note . . . .

Figure 5-11 shows the interventionist's notes for the interventions tried and results section.

**Figure 5-11**

> **I**nterventions Tried and Their Results
>
> Description:
>   Ms. Quivey, grade 3—positive attention and ignoring
>
> How long attempted? 4 weeks
>
> How successful? Positive attention may be helping. Behavior during class is not so disruptive that it can't be ignored by the teacher and students. Last year: special attention—reports and responsibilities, time-out in office—effective to some degree.

# Completing Stage 2: Preparation

In Stage 2, the intervention planning participants work together to specify the desired goal(s) or outcome(s) of the intervention, and explore strategies that may be incorporated into the final plan.

## Goal or Desired Outcome for the Intervention

Use the background information—including the expectations of the student, parent(s), and teacher(s)—to determine the focus of the intervention plan. What will the student be doing differently if the plan is successful?

When determining the goal(s) of the intervention, keep the following guidelines in mind:

- Identify goals that will assist the student in becoming more successful.

  When objectives vary, try to arrive at common goals for the student. If a teacher had hoped to get a student out of her room, careful consideration must be given to reducing the behavior the teacher cannot tolerate. "The goal of the intervention is to have Jeremiah stay in his seat, keep his hands and feet to himself, and to listen attentively during class discussions."

- Identify objectives that will allow the student to focus on one or two areas of improvement.

  With multidimensional problems, limit the scope of what everyone hopes to accomplish. For example, if a student needs to get to get to school on time, use better hygiene, stay on task, learn to complete academic work, learn new social skills with peers, *and* learn to work cooperatively in the classroom, setting intervention goals for everything at once would be overwhelming. By narrowing the objectives, troubled students have a greater chance of success. Once success is experienced, many secondary problems resolve themselves and/or the positive momentum makes the other problems more amenable to future intervention efforts.

- Identify obtainable goals.

  The degree of change desired might also require adjustment. Overly ambitious initial goals might be revised to reflect more intermediary goals. Rather than expecting a highly immature student to become responsible for his behavior within an unstructured room, an intermediary goal might be for the student to be more self-directed during structured activities. "During centers, the student will be assigned to do specific center work, rather than allowing free choice. The student will go directly to the assigned center and follow directions. During center time, the student will stay on task. If work is finished early, he will return to his seat and read in his SSR book."

- When possible, identify specific goals.

  Work for clarity. The more specific the goals, the easier it will be to design an effective intervention. Stating timelines and degrees of goal accomplishment can be useful. For example, if a student has fits of anger and tantrums ten to fifteen times a day, it would be unrealistic to try to eliminate all tantrumming within a week—success would be impossible. Instead, the goal might be to reduce the average number of tantrums each week for the remainder of the year. Following are a few examples of possible goal statements with timelines:

- Within four weeks, the student will be completing at least 80% of her class work.
- Within two weeks, the number of disruptive acts will be reduced by 50%, and within two months, the disruptive acts will be reduced by 80%.
- The student will learn to stay calm and manage her anger without screaming, hitting, or engaging in aggressive acts. Each month, the average number of disruptive incidents will be less than the previous month.

Stating the goal of the intervention in observable and measurable terms establishes criteria that the interventionist and referring teacher can use to determine the success or failure of the intervention.

| | |
|---|---|
| Interventionist: | *Marge, earlier we discussed your overall goals for Travis. Now we need to decide on specific goals for Travis. The more specific we are the better.* |
| Teacher: | *When we started this, I think I wanted Travis to learn to get attention through more positive behavior.* |
| Principal: | *I wonder if we want Travis to get along with other students by talking and playing respectfully with them. He can show he is doing that by reducing his annoying behavior like pushing others' things off desks and harassing others physically. It's kind of broad, but I think it's possible.* |
| Teacher: | *I'd like to get something in there about helping Travis value himself. I don't think he recognizes his strengths. He is such a good student. He is a good athlete. I hate to see all of that go to waste. Learning to value himself isn't very specific, but I really want to lobby for that goal.* |
| Interventionist: | *Travis' statements about himself, and whether he acts out of a sense of competence or a sense of incompetence are essential. Let's put that down along with Arnie's statement.* |

Figure 5-12 shows the interventionist's notes for the goal section.

**Figure 5-12**

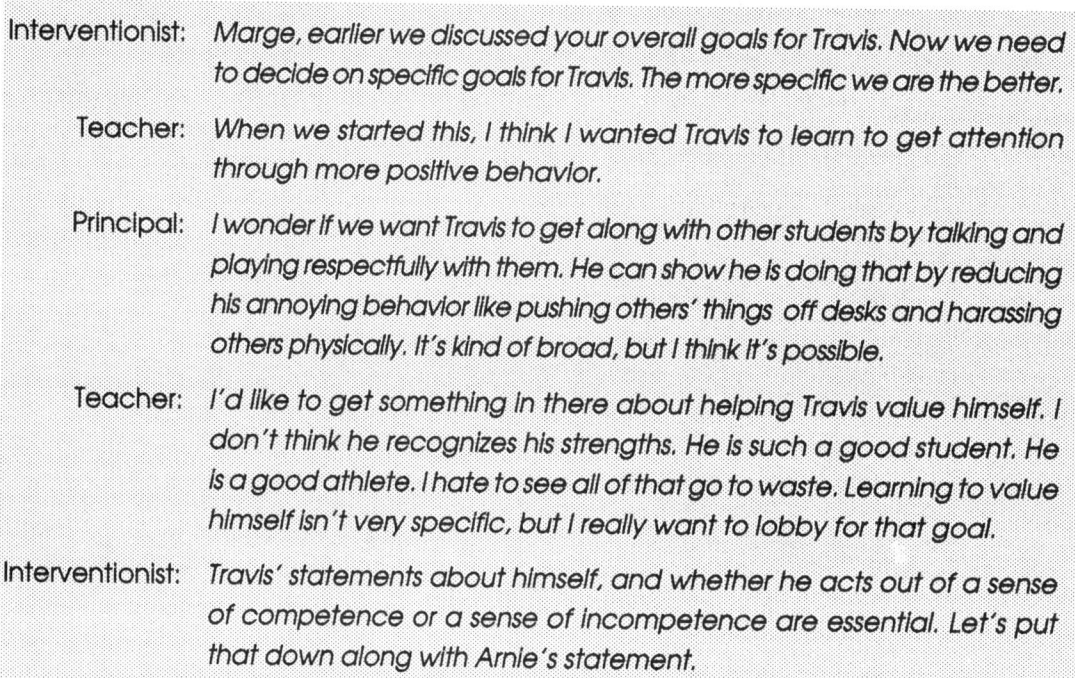

### Stage 2: Preparation

**Goal or Desired Outcome for the Intervention**

-Travis will learn to value his strengths and the importance of being himself.
-Travis will learn to interact positively with other students by talking and playing respectfully and avoiding inappropriate physical behavior like pushing things off desks, grabbing at and poking others, and making hurtful comments.

# Chapter 5
## The In-Depth Intervention Decision Guide (IDG) Process

### Possible Interventions to Consider

Once goal(s) have been established, begin the process of identifying possible interventions using the intervention decision chart provided on the "IDG" form. The decision chart includes: (1) a problem descriptor, in column one; (2) a corresponding intervention strategy, described in intervention booklet form, in column two; (3) a place to check whether the intervention should be considered during intervention planning, in column three; and (4) a place to check if the intervention has been selected for final consideration, in column four. Figure 5-13 shows the completed decision chart for this chapter's scenario.

**Figure 5-13**

| Descriptor (If the statement is true, consider including this intervention as part of the plan.) | | Intervention | Check the intervention(s) to consider. | Check the intervention(s) selected. |
|---|---|---|---|---|
| The behavior poses a threat to someone's physical safety. | | **Intervention A:** *Managing Physically Dangerous Behavior* | | |
| The behavior is so severe that the teacher cannot continue to teach. | | **Intervention B:** *Managing Severely Disruptive Behavior* | | |
| The student may not know what is expected. | | **Intervention C:** *Planned Discussions* | | |
| The student may have an underlying academic problem. | | **Intervention D:** *Academic Assistance* | | |
| The student makes negative comments about himself/herself and/or others. | Maybe | **Intervention E:** *Restructuring Self-Talk* | ✓ | |
| The student seems to be unaware of when he/she engages in inappropriate behavior. | No | **Intervention F:** *Signal Interference Cueing* | ? | |
| The student would benefit from additional adult support and attention. | Yes | **Intervention G:** *Mentoring* | ✓ | ✓ |
| The student is impulsive and has difficulty maintaining emotional control. | | **Intervention H:** *Self-Control Training* | ? | |
| The student has difficulty with motivation and may not understand how to reach a goal. | Yes | **Intervention I:** *Goal Setting and Contracting* | ✓ | |
| The student does not know how to meet expectations. | | **Intervention J:** *Teaching Desired Behaviors* | | |
| The student has some motivation to change or learn new behaviors. | Yes | **Intervention K:** *Self-Monitoring* | ✓ | ✓ |
| The misbehavior is a *firmly* established part of the student's behavior. | No | **Intervention L:** *Structured Reinforcement Systems* | ✓ | |
| The teacher(s) feel anxious, worried, discouraged, or angry about a student or students. | | **Intervention M:** *Managing Stress* | | |
| Several students in a class have difficulty managing their behavior. | | **Intervention N:** *Classroom Management Strategies* | | |
| The student gets a lot of attention from adults and/or peers for misbehavior or failure. | Yes | **Intervention O:** *Increasing Positive Interactions* | ✓ | ✓ |
| It is difficult to be consistent with the student because it is not always clear when the student has crossed the line between appropriate and inappropriate behavior. and/or Consequences for misbehavior seem necessary, but do not seem to work. | Done | **Intervention P:** *Borderlines and Consequences* | ✓ | |

Columns one and three are used to generate an initial list of possible interventions to implement. First, each of the problem descriptors in column one is considered. If a descriptor matches the student's characteristics, a check mark is written in column three. In most cases, this process will result in a range of three to fifteen potential interventions.

> **Interventionist:** *Now we need to identify interventions that might be helpful. Look at the descriptors in the first column of the chart. The first two aren't applicable; Travis does not pose a physical threat and Marge is able to continue teaching through most of his misbehavior. Look at the third descriptor. Do you think Travis knows what is expected?*
>
> **Teacher:** *Oh, yes. That's not a problem.*
>
> **Interventionist:** *We also know that academics are not a problem. Look at the next one. Does Travis make negative comments about himself or others?*
>
> **Teacher:** *Yes.*
>
> **Interventionist:** *Okay, I'll put a check in column three for that one. Intervention E: Restructuring Self-Talk may be a possible intervention.*
>
> **Teacher:** *How about 'The student seems to be unaware of when he/she engages in inappropriate behavior.' You know, I'm not sure—Travis' behavior towards the other kids may be somewhat impulsive.*
>
> **Interventionist:** *Let's put a question mark in column three for Intervention F: Signal Interference Cueing . . . .*

The next step is to determine which of the interventions checked might be considered for the actual implementation plan. Choosing appropriate and effective interventions requires a thorough knowledge of the interventions themselves. Therefore, the interventionist or interventionist and teacher may wish to take a day or two at this point to become more familiar with the individual intervention booklets. Reproducible summary forms are provided at the end of each intervention booklet. A simple way for the interventionist or teacher to become familiar with the sixteen program interventions is to skim the summaries and then choose specific booklets to read. (The audio cassette tapes that are available to accompany this program also highlight the important steps in each intervention and provide another source for becoming acquainted with the sixteen interventions selected for this program.)

When selecting interventions to implement, the intervention planning participants should determine whether the intervention is related to the identified goal(s) or desired outcome(s). Next, it should be determined whether the intervention seems manageable and is appropriate to the situation and student. Finally, the following (and sometimes competing) variables should be balanced:

- The amount of time and effort required of the teacher.

    Even the most cooperative teachers are likely to be overwhelmed by interventions that are too difficult to manage. Classroom teachers cannot ignore the needs of their other students or the normal responsibilities of teaching to manage an individual intervention plan. Furthermore, the ability of teachers to implement strategies varies. When considering an intervention, think about how "intrusive" (i.e., how much teacher time and effort will be required) it is. For example, in most cases Intervention F: *Signal Interference Cueing* is a simple, intervention that does not require a great deal of time and is very easy for the teacher to implement. "It will be very easy for me to cue Casey. If she begins to whine, I can just put my finger to my lips." For some problems, however, signal interference cueing may require the teacher to be extremely vigilant. "To cue Eric, I would need to watch to see when he begins to fidget. As nice as it would be to stop his tantrums early in the cycle, I honestly don't think I could monitor that." If an intervention seems unwieldy, or if it would unduly stress the teacher, it would not be wise to select that intervention.

Related to this factor is a teacher's readiness to work on an intervention. The interventionist should try to assess how frustrated the teacher is with the student and the problem situation. The greater the degree of teacher frustration, the more the interventionist should look for interventions that do not require too much work from the teacher.

- The amount of support available to the teacher.

Even interventions that seem unmanageable for the teacher may be possible to implement given the right resources. One way to avoid overburdening a classroom teacher is to have an administrator, a special education teacher, a counselor, a school psychologist, a well-trained teacher assistant, or the interventionist implement the more highly structured interventions. If Intervention F: *Signal Interference Cueing* is not manageable for the teacher, maybe an aide could cue the student. If Intervention J: *Teaching Desired Behaviors* seems to have a high probability of success, the interventionist might be able to conduct the daily lessons if the classroom teacher cannot.

- The degree of student responsibility and motivation.

Interventions that encourage students to assume the greatest amount of responsibility for change, but that also provide enough support and structure for success, should be selected:

– High Structure Interventions

Some interventions provide high degrees of structure for supporting student success. These interventions tend to require more support and effort from the teacher and other adults involved. More time is required to set up, implement, monitor, and fade the intervention. However, because of the structure and support provided, there is a higher probability of success. Highly structured interventions are appropriate when students have a long history of problem behavior, and/or are involved in fairly severe problems that are likely to be resistant to change. For example, a severely disruptive student may not change his behavior based on the low structure provided by Intervention C: *Planned Discussions*. However, this same student might respond very well to Intervention L: *Structured Reinforcement Systems*.

– Low Structure Interventions

Some interventions provide less structure for supporting student success. These interventions tend to require less time to set up, implement, monitor, and fade. Because students are required to take more responsibility for themselves with these interventions, they are more likely to attribute their success to their own abilities, rather than feeling that adults made them change. Low structure interventions tend to be appropriate for relatively mild misbehavior—behavior that does not require a large change from a student or behavior that the student would be motivated to change. For example, if a student interacts inappropriately with peers, but is motivated to change—wants to make friends and be like the other students—Intervention K: *Self-Monitoring* along with instruction on how to interact with peers might be appropriate. On the other hand, if the student does not seem to care whether the other students enjoy him or not, Intervention L: *Structured Reinforcement Systems* along with instruction on how to interact with peers might be a better choice.

The chart shown in Figure 5-14 provides a guide for determining whether an intervention provides low, medium, or high structure. Some interventions fit more than one category, depending on how the intervention is designed and implemented.

**Figure 5-14: Structure Level of Program Interventions**

| Low Structure | Medium Structure | High Structure |
|---|---|---|
| | | A: *Managing Physically Dangerous Behavior* |
| | | B: *Managing Severely Disruptive Behavior* |
| C: *Planned Discussions* | | |
| | D: *Academic Assistance* | D: *Academic Assistance* |
| | E: *Restructuring Self-Talk* | |
| | F: *Signal Interference Cueing* | |
| G: *Mentoring* | | |
| | | H: *Self-Control Training* |
| I: *Goal Setting and Contracting* | I: *Goal Setting and Contracting* | I: *Goal Setting and Contracting* |
| | | J: *Teaching Desired Behaviors* |
| | K: *Self-Monitoring* | |
| | | L: *Structured Reinforcement Systems* |
| M: *Managing Stress* | | |
| | N: *Classroom Management Strategies* | |
| | O: *Increasing Positive Interactions* | |
| | | P: *Borderlines and Consequences* |

# Chapter 5
## The In-Depth Intervention Decision Guide (IDG) Process

After reviewing the interventions—weighing the advantages and disadvantages of each, select one to four that may be included in the final intervention plan. Put a check mark in column four of the intervention decision chart on the "IDG" form that corresponds to each intervention selected for inclusion in the final plan.

> **Interventionist:** Now for the hard part. We need to narrow down our choices. Let's go back to the goals. We want Travis to value his strengths and the importance of being himself and to learn to interact more respectfully with other students.
>
> **Teacher:** This is going to be hard.
>
> **Interventionist:** As we're going through these, you might want to jot notes in column two by the various interventions on your copy of the 'IDG' form. Then we'll be able to make some decisions. What do you think about Intervention E: _Restructuring Self-Talk_?
>
> **Teacher:** It does have a lot to do with the goal. We want Travis to think and talk more positively. That has to do with valuing himself.
>
> **Interventionist:** I'm going to put a 'maybe' by _Restructuring Self-Talk_, but we don't have to implement it. We'll decide on the final plan in the next step. How about Intervention F: _Signal Interference Cueing_?
>
> **Teacher:** I don't know what that is.
>
> **Interventionist:** Well, in _Signal Interference Cueing_, you or someone else would cue Travis whenever you saw him begin to get involved in inappropriate behavior. Then we would teach him to engage in alternative behavior.
>
> **Teacher:** For the problems we're talking about, I don't think that would apply. I don't think I could catch him at the right time. A lot of the harassment occurs when adults can't closely monitor.
>
> **Interventionist:** I'm going to put a 'no' by _Signal Interference Cueing_.
>
> **Teacher:** I'm interested in the next one—Intervention G: _Mentoring_. Tell me about that.
>
> **Interventionist:** _Mentoring_ involves pairing Travis with a caring adult. The mentor would meet with Travis on a regular schedule kind of like a 'big brother' program. In this case, the mentor might talk to Travis about his school work, or do something athletically with him.
>
> **Principal:** Knowing the family background and Travis, I'd love to see this one implemented. As Marge said earlier, Travis is just a needy kid. Whenever I see him, he sticks to me like glue and most of my contact with him has been in the context of discipline. This one would help with our goal of helping him value himself.

> As they discuss the list of interventions to consider, the group narrows the choices to *Restructuring Self-Talk, Mentoring, Goal Setting and Contracting, Self-Monitoring,* and *Increasing Positive Interactions.*

# Completing Stage 3: Intervention Design

In Stage 3, the final intervention plan is tailored to meet the needs of the particular situation. There are three distinct parts to this stage: (1) the specification of selected interventions; (2) a summary of responsibilities for implementation; and (3) specification of evaluation procedures to determine the effectiveness of the intervention.

## Selected Intervention(s)

In this step, the final selection of intervention(s) is made. This may involve reducing the number of interventions selected to ensure manageability or including strategies not listed on the "IDG" form. Once the final intervention(s) have been selected, make a note of each intervention, its purpose, and how it will be applied to the situation. For example, if *Restructuring Self-Talk* is selected, the note might read *"Restructuring Self-Talk* will be implemented to help the student improve his self-concept."

**Interventionist:** *Well, we've narrowed our list to Restructuring Self-Talk, Mentoring, Goal Setting and Contracting, Self-Monitoring,* and *Increasing Positive Interactions. Let's go ahead and finalize our plan. We're going to need to narrow this down a bit more for the final plan.*

**Teacher:** *Travis could probably benefit from all of these.*

**Interventionist:** *I think you're right, but we need to set up something manageable. Given the family background and the need for Travis to value himself, I think we all agree that we would definitely like to see Mentoring.*

**Teacher:** *Increasing Positive Interactions doesn't take much time or extra preparation, and it's something we could all work on. Arnie, your stopping by to see Travis would be an example.*

**Interventionist:** *Yes, I think we could implement both Mentoring and Increasing Positive Interactions as strategies to help Travis improve his self-concept. We have Restructuring Self-Talk, Goal Setting and Contracting, and Self-Monitoring left, and we need something that will help Travis learn to play and work more respectfully with his peers. I wonder about Self-Monitoring. Restructuring Self-Talk may not be necessary.*

*I could set up a self-monitoring system; it can be used for any behavior. In Travis' case, I think we'd like him to monitor his peer interactions. I'll*

> |                  | need to do some thinking about it, but maybe we could have him rate his own behavior during different parts of the day. |
> |---|---|
> | Teacher: | That sounds good. I could learn about it too. |
> | Interventionist: | What about <u>Goal Setting and Contracting</u>? |
> | Teacher: | Let's hold that in reserve. I'm afraid we might try to do too much. I want to help Travis, but I also know my limits. |
> | Interventionist: | I'm a little worried that we're biting off too much as it is. When we go to the next step and summarize our responsibilities, let's make sure we can handle all of this. |

Figure 5-15 shows the interventionist's notes for the selected interventions section.

**Figure 5-15**

---

### Stage 3: Intervention Design

**Selected Intervention(s)**

- Intervention G: Mentoring to help Travis learn to value himself as a person.
- Intervention O: Increasing Positive Interactions to help Travis learn to get attention positively rather than negatively.
- Intervention K: Self-Monitoring to help Travis learn to engage in positive and respectful interactions with his peers.

---

## Summary of Responsibilities for Implementing the Plan

At this point, the group should carefully review the responsibilities they are about to undertake and flesh out the plan. The recorder should jot down notes about who is responsible for the various aspects of the plan, and timelines for implementation. These notes should be transcribed later by the interventionist and a copy given to each person responsible for implementing the plan.

Figure 5-16 shows the interventionist's notes for the summary of responsibilities section.

**Figure 5-16**

---

**Summary of Responsibilities for Implementing the Plan**

Specify who is responsible for doing what. Establish timelines for implementation.

Intervention G: Mentoring—Arnie will find someone to be Travis' mentor by October 25 and determine a mentor schedule by the week of Nov. 1.

Intervention O: Increasing Positive Interactions—Arnie will stop by to see Travis every other week; no specific time, but will keep track in his calendar.

By Oct. 19:

-Dan will set Travis up to read to first graders once each week after lunch.

-Marge will set up special reports for Travis, and spend one recess each week working with him.

-Marge will make it a point to have a private chit-chat with Travis once each day—noted in her lesson plan book.

Intervention K: Self-Monitoring—By Oct. 19, Dan will develop a self-monitoring system for the meeting with Travis on Oct. 20.

Oct. 20—Dan and Marge will conference with Travis—introducing the self-monitoring system. (Dan will role play positive interactions and negative interactions so that Travis can clearly distinguish between the two.)

Misc.—By Oct. 17, Dan will contact Travis' mother and fill her in on the plan.

---

## Methods for Evaluating Intervention Effectiveness

In this step, participants in the planning process identify procedures to determine whether or not the intervention plan is working. It is easy to view evaluation procedures as a waste of time and energy—an extra layer of work placed on already burdened schedules. However, without designated methods for evaluating the intervention plan, effectiveness tends to be determined solely by teacher perceptions. A teacher who is actively doing something may feel that the plan is working when in fact the student may be misbehaving as often as in the past. In addition to ineffective plans being maintained without useful results, effective procedures may be abandoned because participants in the plan are too close to the situation to see progress. Without evaluation procedures, the effectiveness of an intervention plan may be subject to how the teacher feels about the student and situation at any particular moment. "Jasmine blew it again this morning. She was back to her old ways—taunting and putting down the other kids. I don't think this plan is working." While this may be an accurate assessment of the moment, it may not take into account that the student has made steady improvement. Abandoning a working plan because of a temporary setback would be unwise.

In order to effectively monitor intervention plans and avoid misperceptions, two independent means of evaluating progress are generally recommended. When selecting evaluation procedures, try not to overburden teachers. Effective evaluation procedures include:

- Subjective Perceptions

    One method of evaluating intervention effectiveness is to gather subjective impressions from the teacher(s), parent(s), and student involved. Is the situation better, the same, or worse? This is the easiest and least time-consuming evaluation procedure. Though subjective perceptions alone are not sufficiently reliable, when used in conjunction with another evaluation procedure a clear picture of the intervention's effectiveness generally emerges.

The plan should specify how, when, and by whom opinions on student progress will be solicited. Anecdotal records and/or interviews provide subjective evaluations. For example, the interventionist might conference with the teacher and student after two, four, and six weeks of implementation to determine how the intervention is working.

- Quality Ratings

  Ratings on the quality of student behavior can provide valuable information. While this procedure has a subjective flavor, the rating scales (e.g., Figure 5-17) are usually accompanied by criteria for judging student behavior.

**Figure 5-17**

| Please rate the student's behavior from 8:30-11:30 A.M. this week. |   |   |   |   |   |
|---|---|---|---|---|---|
| **Behavior: Following Directions** |   |   |   |   |   |
| 5 = Followed all directions pleasantly and cooperatively. 3 = Followed most directions pleasantly and cooperatively. 1 = Uncooperative—failed to follow directions. |   |   |   |   |   |
| Monday | 1 | 2 | 3 | 4 | 5 |
| Tuesday | 1 | 2 | 3 | 4 | 5 |
| Wednesday | 1 | 2 | 3 | 4 | 5 |
| Thursday | 1 | 2 | 3 | 4 | 5 |
| Friday | 1 | 2 | 3 | 4 | 5 |

- Work Products

  When the goal of an intervention is to increase the quality or quantity of student work, the evaluation procedures should include some consideration of student work. The records used could be the percentage of assignments completed, scores on tests, grades, number of words written in a journal, and so on. In most cases, this does not require additional work for teachers, only periodic analysis of data already collected.

- Self-Monitoring Data

  Some intervention plans will involve some form of student self-monitoring. For example, a student might record the number of times he raises his hand and the number of times he blurts out in class without raising his hand. Data the student collects can be used to ascertain improvement. If initial data showed that the student blurted out answers ten times during a half hour discussion and never raised his hand, a self-monitoring system that showed that the student raised his hand 50% of the time and blurted out responses 50% of the time would indicate clear progress.

- Data From a Reinforcement System

  If the intervention plan includes a reinforcement system, the reinforcement system itself will provide information on the effectiveness of the intervention. The plan will include a method for determining whether the student earns a reinforcer. For example, the teacher may give the student a "+" for every fifteen minute period the student behaved positively, and a "-" for every fifteen minute period that the student engaged in misbehavior. The total number of pluses and minuses could be charted each day, to show the student's degree of success. (See Intervention L: *Structured Reinforcement Systems*.)

- Data Collected During an Observation

  Observations can yield information regarding the frequency of a behavior, the amount of time the student engages in a behavior, the length of time it takes between a stimulus and when a student engages in a behavior, and/or the intensity and quality of a behavior. Each of these procedures yields important objective data to help evaluate the effectiveness of an intervention. An observation or observations should be scheduled before an intervention is implemented, and then periodically following the implementation of the intervention. Observations conducted by outside observers should be scheduled for times when the student has the greatest difficulty, with follow-up observations scheduled for the same times and for the same lengths of time.

  The types of data collected during the observations could include the following:

  - **Frequency Data.** During an observation, a count can be taken of whenever a student engages in a particular behavior (e.g., the number of times the student gets out of her seat in a day, or the number of times the student interacts with the teacher disrespectfully). An outside observer might make a simple tally of the number of times the student engages in the behavior. When the observer is keeping an anecdotal record of student behavior, the count of the targeted behavior can be made after the observation.

  - **Time Associated With Behaviors.** Evaluation information might also include the amount of time a student engages in a particular behavior (duration). For example, if a student engages in tantrums, the teacher might record the number of tantrums (a frequency count) and use a stop watch to keep track of the amount of time the student spent tantrumming. By the end of the day, the stop watch would show the accumulated amount of time the student spent tantrumming. "Trent tantrummed three times today for a total of 58 minutes."

    Sometimes it is appropriate to note the amount of time it takes for a particular behavior to begin after a stimulus (latency). For example, if a student has trouble following the teacher's directions, it may be appropriate to record the length of time between when an instruction is given and when the student begins to comply.

  Though observations are generally associated with outside observers, the teacher is a constant observer of student behavior. If time allows, the teacher can take very accurate data on student behavior. To take frequency data, for example, a teacher might carry a small index card in his pocket. Whenever the student engages in the targeted behavior, the teacher makes a tally mark on the card. If the student engages in tantrums, the teacher might keep a simple record of tantrums per day on a calendar.

# Chapter 5
## The In-Depth Intervention Decision Guide (IDG) Process

- Audio or Video Records

    Audio or video tapes can provide effective documentation of changes in student behavior. Recordings would be made both before the intervention is implemented and then at periodic intervals after implementation. Pre- and postintervention tapes could be examined to determine whether there are qualitative and/or quantitative changes in student behavior. Frequency, duration, and latency data can be obtained from the recordings.

Interventions rarely run a smooth and gradual course toward success; therefore, trends are important when determining whether an intervention is having a positive effect on student behavior. Charting data can be very useful for recognizing trends in student behavior. Types of behavior that can be counted and charted include:

- The number of times each day the student uses profanity;
- The number of minutes spent in time-out each day;
- The total number of minutes owed for delaying following an instruction;
- The number of pluses earned during the day, representing ten minute periods of time on task;
- Average ratings of "How hard I worked" for fifteen minute periods throughout the school day; and
- Percentage of assignments completed.

Charts visually depict trends and help teachers determine whether their subjective impressions match what's actually happening. When a student's behavior is especially stressful for a teacher, data may be needed to help the teacher recognize progress. If a teacher is feeling despair, burn out, or a sense that his efforts are not making a difference, this information can reinforce the teacher to continue his efforts. Figure 5-18 shows a sample frequency of a student's angry outbursts. The student has good days and bad days, but on the average his behavior is improving.

**Figure 5-18**

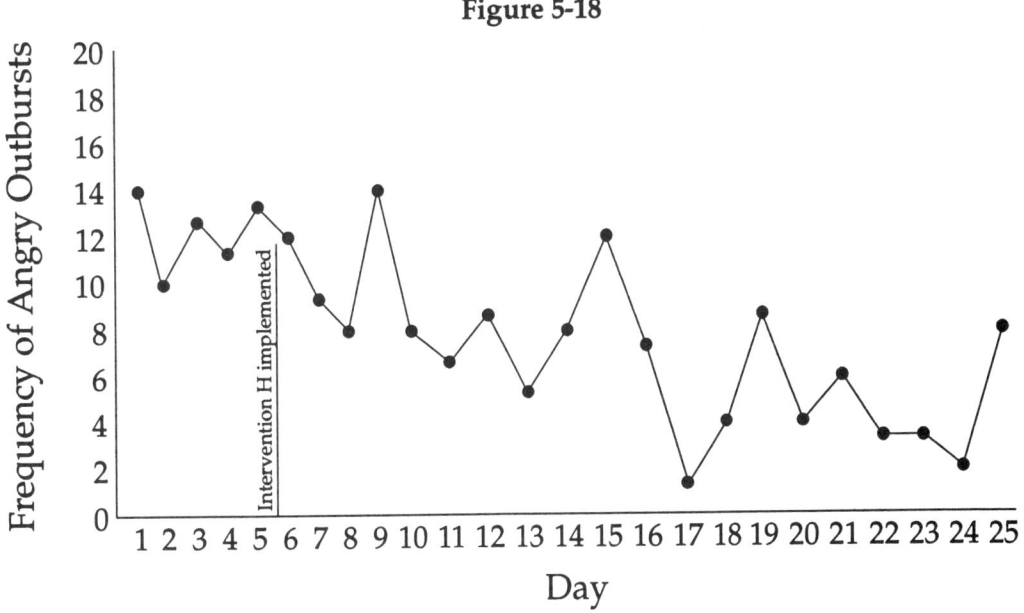

Procedural Manual

> Interventionist: I am very excited about this plan for Travis. Given what Arnie has told us, Travis has already made progress since last year. We are almost ready to implement the plan. Now we need to figure out one last thing—how we're going to evaluate the plan. Whatever we do needs to be pretty simple.
>
> Teacher: Good. So far we're okay, so let's not complicate things.
>
> Interventionist: We can use Travis' self-monitoring system. Then, we need one other way to evaluate how things are going. Marge, how would it be if I had you rate Travis' behavior at the end of each day? We could rig up a little evaluation scale that was similar to Travis'. It would only take you a minute at the end of the day to fill out. Both procedures are somewhat subjective, but they should give us the information we need. If we decide we need something more objective, we can always add independent observations later.
>
> Teacher: I could handle that.

Figure 5-19 shows the interventionist's notes for the methods for evaluating section.

**Figure 5-19**

---
**Methods for Evaluating Intervention Effectiveness**
Specify at least two sources of evaluation information.
- Student's self-monitoring system
- Daily teacher rating—based on system similar to the student's, but for the whole day
---

Before the intervention design stage is complete, the first formal follow-up should be scheduled.

> Interventionist: Great, we've got our plan then. Marge, I'd like to meet about a week after we get this started.
>
> Teacher: That's fine. We could meet during my morning break if you're free or before school sometime.
>
> Interventionist: It shouldn't take long. How about Tuesday, Oct. 26 at 8:00 A.M. in your room?

Once the plan is finalized, the interventionist should ask the participants if there are any questions, and indicate that a written summary of the plan with each person's responsibilities listed will be distributed to all relevant participants. The meeting should be concluded with words of encouragement and thanks to the participants for their assistance.

## Summary of Final Plan

To close the planning process, the interventionist should summarize the plan in writing, listing each person's responsibilities. Good intentions and the best laid plans are easily waylaid by confusion or forgetfulness. The summary sheet (see Figure 5-20) will assist in keeping the participants on track.

Figure 5-20

### Intervention Sheet Summary

| Date | 10/12 | | |
|---|---|---|---|
| Student(s) | Travis Gregerson | Age 9 | Grade 4 |
| Teacher(s) | Marge Quivey | | |
| Other Participants | Dan Kameenui (interventionist), Arnie Smith (principal) | | |

**Goal(s)** To learn to value his strengths and the importance of being himself.
To learn to interact positively with other students by talking and playing respectfully and avoiding inappropriate behavior like pushing things off desks, grabbing at and poking others, and making hurtful comments.

| Date | Action(s) | Responsibility |
|---|---|---|
| By Oct. 15 | Contact Mrs. Gregerson. | Dan will call. |
| Beginning the week of Oct. 18 | Arnie will stop in to see Travis once per week, keeping track on his calendar. | Arnie will keep track in his calendar. |
| | Travis will read to first grade students once per week. | Dan will set up with first grade teacher. |
| | Private chat with Travis each day. | Marge will keep track in her lesson plan book. |
| Oct. 19 | Design of self-monitoring system for peer interactions | Dan will set up. |
| Oct. 20 | Conference with Travis at noon.<br>-Teach Travis and Marge how to use the self-monitoring system. | Marge and Dan<br>Dan |
| | Marge will check with Travis before each recess to see how self-monitoring is going. | Marge |
| Oct. 21 | Initial follow-up | Dan will check in with Marge and Travis during the day following implementation. |
| Beginning the week of Oct. 25 | Marge will set up special reports for Travis. | Marge |
| Oct. 26 | Follow-up meeting #1 at 8:00 A.M., Room 15 | Marge and Dan |
| | Marge—Let me know if you need help!<br>—Dan | |

NOTE: *A copy of this form is provided in the "Reproducible Materials" at the end of this manual.*

# Completing Stage 4: Implementation

The "IDG" form has set the stage for a carefully designed intervention plan. During implementation, it is important for all the adults to follow through with their responsibilities. The support provided by the planning participants can make the difference in whether an intervention plan works or not.

## Initial Follow-Up Notes

After the first day of implementation, the interventionist conducts a quick "check-up" with the teacher. This way, if there are any glitches in the plan or procedures that require clarification, they can be taken care of quickly.

> **Interventionist:** *Marge, just thought I'd check to see how things went yesterday with Travis' self-monitoring system.*
>
> **Teacher:** *It went pretty well. The only glitch we had was knowing how to evaluate a few times.*
>
> **Interventionist:** *Why don't I pop in for a few minutes tomorrow and I can monitor? We may need to work on our descriptors a little.*
>
> **Teacher:** *That would be great. Any time is fine. Travis is taking this very seriously. I think he wants the other kids to like him.*

Figure 5-21 shows the interventionist's notes for the initial follow-up section.

**Figure 5-21**

---
### Stage 4: Implementation

*I*nitial Follow-Up Notes

Oct. 21—Minor fine tuning of self-monitoring descriptors.
Extra role playing with Travis scheduled for ten minutes on Oct. 22, 23, and 24
---

## Follow-Up #1

During Follow-Up # 1, the interventionist and teacher evaluate the student's progress and make modifications to the plan if necessary. Guidelines for maintaining, modifying, and fading intervention plans include:

- Develop a new intervention plan if the student makes no progress or gets worse.

    When the student shows no progress, the plan may need to be redesigned. However, before abandoning a plan, there should be two independent means of verifying that the plan is not working. For example, if a student has been making steady progress, but "blows it" one day, the teacher may feel that the student hasn't made any progress at all. Evaluation information and the support of the interventionist can help the teacher and student stay on course.

# Chapter 5
## The In-Depth Intervention Decision Guide (IDG) Process

- Modify the intervention plan to provide more support and structure if progress is very slow or has come to a halt.

  Because intervention planning involves trial and error, it may become apparent that the student requires more assistance.

- Maintain the intervention plan if the student is making good progress.

  If the student is making steady progress towards a goal, the plan should be maintained until the student demonstrates continuous success in achieving the goal.

- Fade the intervention plan when there is a high probability that the student can maintain success.

  Fading is accomplished by gradually providing less structure and support. Some intervention plans are automatically faded as the student becomes successful. For example, signal interference would be used less and less as a student demonstrated success. Eventually, the cueing would be faded completely.

> **Interventionist:** *How are things going?*
>
> **Teacher:** *Yesterday we had one of those 'good ol' days' and I was feeling kind of discouraged, but as I look at my daily ratings I can see that Travis just had a bad day. We haven't hit any 5s yet (goal accomplished), but he is hitting 4s most days. So, he is doing better.*
>
> **Interventionist:** *That's good to hear. I'll keep a record of your daily ratings on a chart if you'd like. We'll want to track them to see whether Travis gradually begins hitting those 5s. How do Travis' charts look?*
>
> **Teacher:** *They look pretty much like mine. I'm amazed at how honest he is in his evaluations. Yesterday he gave himself a 2 and that was what I did too.*
>
> **Interventionist:** *What do you think? Shall we stay the course?*
>
> **Teacher:** *Yes, I'm sure this is helping. Do you think he'll grow bored with this?*
>
> **Interventionist:** *Let's watch the chart. You'll also be starting his special report writing next week. I'd like to see him sort of outgrow this, but I don't want to rush it. Let's set a time for a second follow-up visit. By then Arnie will have also gotten mentoring started.*

Figure 5-22 shows the interventionist's notes for the first follow-up section.

**Figure 5-22**

---
*Follow-Up #1*

    Date of the follow-up meeting: 10/26

    Purpose of the follow-up meeting: Determine whether the intervention is helping Travis with interactions and self-esteem

    Summary of the follow-up meeting: Good progress—intervention will be continued as planned.
---

## Follow-Up #2

The second formal follow-up conference should be conducted much like the first, with an emphasis on determining whether the intervention should be maintained, modified, or faded.

## Providing Long-Term Follow-Up

Intervention plans are more often successful when a focus on the goal(s) can be maintained over time. For students with chronic to severe behavior problems, intervention may shift from highly structured interventions to less structured assistance. However, at-risk students generally need ongoing assistance. If there are temporary setbacks, someone must be there to help the students get back on track. At-risk students need to be shown again and again that they can learn from their mistakes. They need to feel confident that someone will always be there to assist them.

| | |
|---|---|
| Interventionist: | Travis, it's nice to see you. How're things going? |
| Student: | Pretty good! |
| Teacher: | Travis is doing really well. His grades are terrific. In fact, we just entered one of his essays in a writing contest. Whether he wins or not, it was a great piece of writing. |
| Interventionist: | I'd like to see it, Travis. |
| Student: | I'll go get it. We kept a copy. |
| Interventionist: | (After Travis leaves . . .) He seems real upbeat. |
| Teacher: | Yes. We continue to work on things. Once in awhile he has a problem, but overall he's made great progress. You know, he's still meeting with Mr. Thompson once a week. I see them shooting baskets. |
| Interventionist: | That's great. What kinds of things does he still have difficulty with? |
| Teacher: | I'm not sure exactly. He and two other kids ended up in Arnie's office yesterday. The other boys said that Travis pushed them when he didn't get his way. He does still have a temper. |
| Interventionist: | I know. It's okay. I just hope he learns to direct it constructively. Do you think he needs some help? |
| Teacher: | Let's ask Travis. |

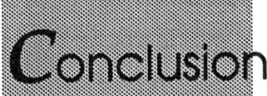

## Conclusion

The Intervention Decision Guide (IDG) process provides collaborative groups with the structure necessary to develop an in-depth intervention plan for problems that are complex and not easily resolved. Through ongoing planning, implementation, and revision of plans, at-risk students can gradually develop the skills and responsibility to be successful in the school setting.

# CHAPTER 6

## Skills of the Interventionist

THE JOB OF an interventionist is complex and challenging. Ensuring high quality services for students, staff members, and families is a difficult task. The skilled interventionist must be knowledgeable about the range of possible interventions. She needs to know which interventions will have the highest probability of success, how to apply procedures to specific situations, and how to combine interventions into multidimensional solutions. However, this technical knowledge, while necessary, is not sufficient to develop the working relationships required to produce and implement effective interventions.

An interventionist functions as an advocate; first and foremost, to safeguard the needs of the student. However, she also serves as an advocate for teachers and families. Therefore, the interventionist must possess the communication, interpersonal, and management skills required to: (1) communicate effectively with staff members, students, and families; (2) recognize and respond to different individuals' strengths, limitations, needs, and biases; and (3) balance competing interests to help people work together through the unique conditions of each problem.

This chapter outlines some basic skills necessary to be an effective interventionist—communication and interpersonal skills and self-evaluation and reflection. Although much of the content is embedded throughout previous chapters and the sixteen program intervention booklets, the information in this chapter may be useful for an interventionist who wishes to review or analyze her own skills and practices.

## Communication and Interpersonal Skills

Learning to communicate effectively is a life-long task. Each situation and every relationship requires specific communication skills and provides a unique opportunity to learn. The effective interventionist continuously fine tunes her ability to collaborate with students, staff members, and parents. The effective interventionist with good communication and interpersonal skills will use the following procedures.

## Active Listening

The skilled interventionist processes and retains what others say to her. She pays attention to the content of what is being said as well as to the tone of voice and body language of the speaker. She asks questions to help her fully understand the problem, and she clarifies and paraphrases what she hears. For example:

- What else did they do?
- You felt angry, but the students seemed to get quiet.
- Why do you think that happened?
- What have you tried so far?
- I'm sure that's frustrating.

Active listening can help an interventionist determine whether a staff member or parent is ready to look at problem resolution or simply wants to vent frustration. Making suggestions too soon tends to elicit "Yeah, but..." responses. If staff members and/or parents aren't given an opportunity to describe the problem and things they've tried, they are bound to feel resentful of the interventionist. "Rebecca just doesn't understand what I have to deal with."

Active listening helps the interventionist create a climate of trust and collaboration.

> Teacher: ... Kent and Barry are probably the toughest of the bunch.
>
> Interventionist: What do they do?
>
> Teacher: They are real leaders, but unfortunately they lead the class in the wrong direction. If I give a direction, they just ignore me. You'd think I was speaking a foreign language.
>
> Interventionist: That would be frustrating. It must make teaching really hard.
>
> Teacher: I'd like to get them split up, but the principal said that they were careful with placements last year, and that neither of the boys would mix any better in any of the other classrooms.
>
> Interventionist: Does it look like you have to live with the situation?
>
> Teacher: Yeah.
>
> Interventionist: Have you found anything that makes a difference?
>
> Teacher: I tried separating the boys. That helps a bit.
>
> Interventionist: Good. Tell me a little more about what they do. Maybe we can put our heads together and come up with some ideas for making this year more livable.

Through active listening, the interventionist may be able to assist with the planning and implementation of interventions that directly help troubled students. Active listening may also result in the interventionist serving as a general resource to teachers who are having difficulties managing a difficult student or students. Sometimes by encouraging teachers to discuss what they would like their classes to be like, strategies can be

# Chapter 6
## Skills of the Interventionist

suggested that will assist in creating that vision. (See Intervention M: *Managing Stress*; Intervention N: *Classroom Management Strategies*; Intervention O: *Increasing Positive Interactions*; and Intervention P: *Borderlines and Consequences*.)

> Interventionist: *It sounds like you've tried a lot of things—keeping the kids in at recess, calling their parents, working on rules with the class . . . I'm sure that it's disappointing when things don't work out.*
>
> Teacher: *It is really frustrating! I got into this profession because I wanted to teach. With this group of kids I feel like I'm a combination babysitter-prison guard. They aren't mature enough, or their values aren't strong enough, to trust them with any kind of responsibility.*
>
> Interventionist: *You do have a challenging group this year. I've worked with several of the kids in the past. The two of us might be able to work out some strategies that would help improve the situation. As you know, there aren't any magic tricks, but we might find some things that would help them gradually move in the right direction.*
>
> Interventionist: *(At a later meeting . . .) How have things been going?*
>
> Teacher: *Actually, not as bad. I talked to Kent about the tutoring he did last year. His eyes lit up and he was almost friendly the rest of the day.*
>
> Interventionist: *That's great. Perhaps things are beginning to turn around a bit.*
>
> Teacher: *I'm not sure it will last, though. One of the other kids began picking on Kent and then we were into problems again. Sometimes it feels like a losing battle with this group.*
>
> Interventionist: *There are a hundred stumbling blocks. A lot of your kids don't have good models at home. If you had the ideal class, what would it be like?*
>
> Teacher: *The ideal class? That's interesting. Hmm . . . It would be a group of kids who respected each other—and me. They would be engaged in their work, take pride in their accomplishments, and have fun.*
>
> Interventionist: *Would you be interested in working together to create that vision? I don't think it's impossible. Hard maybe, but together we might be able to turn this whole group around. I have two or three intervention booklets in mind that we might study together. We could sift through the strategies and pick some that might have merit.*

## Use of Everyday Language When Discussing Problems and Sharing Perceptions

The skilled interventionist is careful to use the language of staff members, parents, and students. Using technical jargon or confusing language may create barriers to collaboration. For example, interventionists with school psychology backgrounds sometimes use words such as "intermittent reinforcement," "antecedent event," and "differential reinforcement of low rates of behavior (DRL)." This vocabulary reflects useful concepts from the science of behaviorism, however these same ideas can be described in everyday language. Contrast the following two statements:

> Interventionist 1: *If you watch Norm carefully, the antecedent event to his agitation seems to be Tasha approaching him. I wonder if we can figure out why.*
>
> Interventionist 2: *If you watch Norm carefully, he seems to get agitated whenever Maya approaches him. I wonder if we can figure out why.*

A teacher listening to Interventionist 1 might be left thinking, "Figure out what? I have no idea what she's talking about!" On the other hand, a teacher working with Interventionist 2 is more likely to respond, "That's interesting. Do you suppose that Norm just doesn't trust adults?"

## A Value-Free Manner of Discussing Problems and Sharing Perceptions

Language that conveys particular biases or philosophies may hinder effective communication. Value-laden terminology can inadvertently create barriers that are difficult to tear down. On the other hand, a discussion focused specifically on the needs of the student is more likely to engage than alienate a teacher. Contrast the following two comments:

> Interventionist 1: *Chris needs a developmentally appropriate environment. She needs to be able to stretch and move physically.*
>
> Interventionist 2: *I wonder if Chris is just one of those kids who is going to have a difficult time staying still. Do you think we could structure her work space so she could move, but not bother the other children?*

The first interventionist risks putting the teacher on the defensive. If the teacher hasn't adopted a "developmentally appropriate" philosophy, she might wonder, "Is the interventionist saying that my classroom is not developmentally appropriate? I think it's developmentally appropriate to teach children to stay on task and not prevent others from working!" In future discussions, the teacher may feel the interventionist is judging her against the unknown standards of "developmentally appropriate" practice.

On the other hand, by keeping the conversation focused on the needs of the student and the situation, the second interventionist involves the teacher in problem solving. "Maybe we could create a space for Chris to move about while she is working, and also teach her not to bother the other students."

# Working With Staff and Parents as a Collaborator Rather Than an "Expert"

The effective interventionist acts as a *resource*. She is there to provide support, assistance, and guidance to teachers, students, and/or families as they design intervention plans. She may ask questions and offer suggestions, but as much as possible she will avoid telling people what they "ought" to do. When an interventionist grandstands, working relationships may be jeopardized and the interests of students sacrificed. The effective interventionist collaborates with others to jointly resolve problems and avoids setting herself up as an "expert." The following quote summarizes the problem with experts.

> Human experts and rabbits have much in common. Firstly, they multiply at a prolific rate. Secondly, they are both highly susceptible to infection; rabbits catch myxomatosis and experts catch expertosis. The symptoms are common to both: The head swells and the patient goes blind.
>
> — Cliff Cunningham
> (Cunningham & Shillington, 1990)

# Sensitivity to the Various Participants During Intervention Planning and Implementation

Each person brings unique characteristics to the situation. Throughout intervention planning and implementation, an interventionist must be sensitive to the needs and abilities of individual students, teachers, and families:

- Through observation, interviews, and assessment, the effective interventionist can develop and provide an objective view of the needs and abilities of each student. During intervention planning and implementation, the interventionist serves an important role—helping to clarify realistic expectations for each student. What works with some students may not work with others.

> **Interventionist:** So, our goal is to help Cindy be more responsible for her work.
>
> **Teacher:** Yes, I really think the problem is that Cindy just doesn't care.
>
> **Interventionist:** I like the idea of teaching Cindy to care about her work. As we look at strategies, we'll need to be careful to determine what she can do. Academics are still very hard for her. June, if you can give us examples of assignments she's had problems with, then we can go through and try to identify whether problems were related to 'can't do' or 'won't do.'
>
> **Teacher:** I guess a good example would be this paper. She was to look up words in the glossary and copy definitions. She lost her place and copied parts of the wrong definition several times.

> Interventionist: Let's take a look at the words and the words in the definitions. You know June, this is just a guess, but I wonder if Cindy understands the words she was copying?
>
> Teacher: Gosh, I hadn't really thought about that. I don't know. I know she can read them.
>
> Interventionist: The glossary has some pretty hard definitions.
>
> Teacher: If that is a problem, what are we going to do?
>
> Interventionist: We're going to have to try to find a balance between teaching Cindy to compensate for her academic problems and providing her with adaptations to the assignments. Perhaps by combining some motivational techniques and adjusting the assignments we can help Cindy care more about her work.

- The effective interventionist is sensitive to the needs of the teacher—providing services prior to intervention, during intervention planning and implementation, and following the intervention. One of the primary roles of the interventionist is to help reduce teacher isolation and to encourage collaboration. Students with behavior problems often create stress for teachers. When dealing with challenging situations, teachers need an opportunity to talk to someone who is not judgmental. An interventionist can help simply by listening to a teacher and discussing a problem.

The interventionist can also protect the teacher if planning becomes unrealistic. Interventionists with regular classroom teaching experience can sometimes anticipate when a teacher may have difficulties implementing an intervention. If an interventionist hasn't had classroom experience, she can actively work at understanding the demands of the classroom and try to anticipate where problems may occur.

> Interventionist: I love this part of the plan, but when I try to imagine my doing this with 25 other children in the room, I think I would forget. Breanna, do you see that as a potential problem?
>
> ----
>
> Interventionist: As I try to envision you doing this when you see 180 kids a day, I wonder if we need to consider an alternative plan, or if we need to find some way to assist you. What do you think?

Through good communication, an interventionist can also help teachers identify what is going well. Working with at-risk students requires patience and endurance. During the many setbacks that are bound to occur, teachers may need assistance recognizing that progress is being made.

> Teacher: Clay really blew it today. I had to send him to the office.
>
> Interventionist: What did he do?

# Chapter 6
## Skills of the Interventionist

| | |
|---|---|
| Teacher: | He started to pull on Malory's pony tail and they got into a major argument. |
| Interventionist: | That must be really frustrating. |
| Teacher: | Do you think what we're doing is really helping? |
| Interventionist: | How long has it been since you had to refer Clay to the office? |
| Teacher: | I don't know. Maybe three or four weeks. It has been a while, hasn't it? |
| Interventionist: | Do you remember what he did that time? |
| Teacher: | That was the time he chased the kids with a pair of scissors. I guess he has made progress, hasn't he? |

- An interventionist must also be sensitive to the needs of different families. What is realistic for one family may be entirely unrealistic for another. It is important for the interventionist to make sure that requests made of a family do not ask more than the family can deliver. She can help the family by providing direct assistance and by offering suggestions.

| | |
|---|---|
| Teacher: | Jordan is failing because he never gets his homework done. He can do the work; he just chooses not to. I think we need to get his parents involved in this. It's their responsibility. |
| Interventionist: | I agree that it's their responsibility to encourage him to complete his homework. Let's brainstorm some other possibilities though. Then we can talk pros and cons. |
| Teacher: | What is there to discuss? You call the parents. If they don't get the kid to do his homework, then it isn't our problem. |
| Interventionist: | I know that this kind of problem is very hard because we want students to assume responsibility for their own work. But the fact is that Jordan hasn't learned to do that and it appears that his parents won't or can't help. I spoke with Jordon's dad last week. He works at night, and it sounds like the mother spends her evenings in the bars. If we both work together, I think we can help Jordan. His parents love him, but neither seems to be able to help right now. The first suggestion I have would be to get Jordan involved in Ala-Teen. |

- Finally, when there are conflicts of interests, the effective interventionist keeps focused on the intervention plan. For example, if a teacher wants a disruptive child out of his classroom, but the interventionist does not feel this is in the best interest of the student, she could handle it as follows:

> **Teacher:** *I really can't tolerate Darren any more. He has disrupted my class more times than I care to remember. He's disrespectful and obnoxious, and I don't want him returned.*
>
> **Interventionist:** *I know that Darren has really caused problems. I am sorry we were not there to help sooner.*
>
> **Teacher:** *I don't think it would have done any good. I've tried everything with that kid and nothing works.*
>
> **Interventionist:** *I'm sure you have. What I'd like to do with you today is go through an intervention plan called <u>Managing Severely Disruptive Behavior</u>. Part of the plan will be to consider special education referral, but also to keep your classroom livable while we are doing that.*

## Guiding the Intervention Process Efficiently

An interventionist often serves as the case manager or facilitator for collaborative problem solving teams (e.g., a teacher and interventionist; a teacher, parent, and interventionist; a Teacher Assistance Team (TAT), a prereferral team, a Care Team, a grade level team, etc.). Regardless of the composition, whenever a group jointly designs and implements an intervention plan, someone must assume responsibility for coordinating the process. The following guidelines for the case manager will assist in the clear communication required for the intervention process to move smoothly.

- Respond promptly to requests for assistance.

   The effective interventionist moves quickly to determine the urgency of a problem once a request for assistance has been made. If the problem involves physically dangerous behavior, it is important to establish emergency procedures without delay (see Intervention A: *Managing Physically Dangerous Behavior*). When the problem is severe—the teacher has "had it" or can't teach—the interventionist should schedule a meeting within a day of the request to determine next steps. For less severe problems, the interventionist should try to schedule a meeting within a week.

- Organize meetings.

   After determining, with the teacher, the format for the intervention planning and who should participate, the interventionist should take responsibility for contacting those involved. Depending on the urgency of the problem, she should provide as much notice as possible.

- Set and maintain a positive tone to the meeting.

   An effective interventionist is not only familiar with the three planning formats presented in Chapters 3, 4, and 5, but also takes an active role in conducting the meetings. The interventionist can set the tone for collaborative meetings by welcoming and introducing each participant.

# Chapter 6
## Skills of the Interventionist

> Interventionist: *Mitchell, I know you've met Gabriel and Lydia Armijo. I appreciate everyone taking the time to meet. I know there have been a lot of phone conversations, and I think it will be good to sit down together.*

The interventionist should also make a statement regarding the purpose of the meeting at the beginning. Conflicts can be prevented when a clear focus on the needs of the student has been established. Briefly acknowledging any past differences and summarizing common goals allows the interventionist to move the discussion directly to productive ground.

> Interventionist: *Despite past differences, we're meeting today to focus on what we can do to help Amelio have a better year. Lydia and Gabriel have shared their concerns with me and I've also spoken with Mitchell. You all have the same goals for Amelio and the class. You'd like to see a respectful atmosphere in the classroom. You'd like to have the kids learn as much as possible, which means that they need to become engaged and to work hard on their assignments and activities in class.*
>
> *Let me explain some of the strategies Mitchell and I are working on to improve the classroom atmosphere. First, Mitchell has designed some classroom rules that we'll share with you. To teach the students how to follow the rules, we have been working on role playing and some other things. Mitchell can explain what we are doing with the whole class.*

- Move meetings along.

  Intervention planning meetings can easily become too lengthy, with inordinate amounts of time spent complaining or hashing and rehashing ideas. Although participants may be enthusiastic during the meeting, later they may resent the amount of time invested. The effective interventionist develops the skill of encouraging involvement, but keeps the discussion focused and moving along. (Both the structured 25 minute planning process and the "Intervention Decision Guide" ("IDG") provide the interventionist a structure to do this.)

- Avoid spending large amounts of time focusing on consequences for misbehavior.

  While consequences are often a necessary part of an intervention plan, they are unlikely to have an effect on problems that involve moderate to severe misbehavior. Usually by the time a teacher makes a referral, the most common consequences for misbehavior have been tried. An effective interventionist will direct the group to put the majority of their time into planning proactive interventions—those that teach the student appropriate behavior—rather than interventions that focus on consequences for the misbehavior.

- Clarify the responsibilities of students, teachers, parents, and others by providing a written summary of the plan.

  The interventionist can facilitate implementation by providing each participant with a written summary of the planning meeting and a list of their responsibilities during implementation. While summarizing plans, the interventionist should watch for inconsistencies, omissions, and potential glitches or places where the participants might need additional assistance. If materials are necessary, the summary should specify them. (Interventionists can help overburdened teachers by providing or developing any materials needed to implement the plan.)

- Make sure the plan is fully understood by all the participants.

  When an intervention is fairly complex or involves new skills, the interventionist can rehearse the plan with the participants. A dry run may help the participants clarify parts of the plan and work out any glitches. The interventionist can also offer to model the new procedures, giving the participants an opportunity to learn by watching.

- Offer support as needed.

  Often it will be the interventionist who presents the plan to a student. The interventionist can answer questions and help the teacher and student work out the details of the plan. She can give examples and have the student and teacher practice or role play relevant parts of the plan. When explaining a plan to a student, the interventionist should have the student paraphrase the information. If the student doesn't have the language skills to paraphrase, the interventionist should ask questions to make sure the student understands the plan.

  Finally, when an intervention plan involves teaching the student a new skill, the interventionist can either provide the instruction or offer to cover the teacher's class while the teacher instructs the student. Sometimes, a student is asked to demonstrate the new skill in context. The interventionist can provide on-site coaching—prompting the student to use the new skill and giving feedback to the student.

- Provide follow-up both during and after intervention implementation.

  The interventionist assumes primary responsibility for monitoring implementation—scheduling brief check-ins, arranging follow-up meetings, evaluating student progress, and supervising decisions to maintain, modify, or fade interventions. The interventionist also usually assumes primary responsibility for postintervention follow-ups. Even when a student has been successful and the intervention is faded, it is important for someone to follow through with both the student and the teacher. Without continued monitoring, the student and teacher may find themselves falling back into old habits. By conducting periodic postintervention follow-ups, the interventionist can provide the support needed to keep the student on track.

# Self-Evaluation and Reflection

In order to enhance her effectiveness, the skilled interventionist continually evaluates her knowledge, the quality of her interpersonal skills, and her ability to help others design and implement successful interventions. As part of this self-evaluation, the effective interventionist engages in reflection—analyzing her goals, activities, and relationships, as well as the outcomes of her collaborative efforts. Some practices used by effective interventionists for reflection include the following.

## Keeping a Confidential Journal

A confidential journal allows an interventionist to record thoughts, impressions, and events that might not be appropriate to keep in a student's file. As the interventionist works on cases, the act of writing provides an opportunity to explore ideas, pose questions, think about possible solutions, and make predictions. While writing, an interventionist can consider why certain procedures were effective or ineffective.

Keeping a journal also provides a vehicle for reviewing cases. Journal entries provide the interventionist a way to examine the accuracy of past predictions and impressions, identify patterns, and track progress. When a journal has been kept over a long time, the interventionist can track her own professional growth.

## Working With a Study Group

An interventionist does not always have others she can talk to about being an interventionist, due to issues of trust and confidentiality. Like other professionals, though, she needs opportunities to talk freely with others who share similar responsibilities. A study group can provide the interventionist with the same support she gives to staff members, students, and parents. The study group can structure a way for the interventionist to meet and share cases, discuss ideas and procedures, explore problems, and celebrate successes.

When school counselors, school psychologists, and special education resource teachers act as interventionists in a district, these professionals might meet in small study groups once per month. The agenda may involve presentations of case studies. Here is a possible agenda for conducting a case study analysis:

1. Briefly present the situation, demographic information, and the reason for the referral. Include the age of the student, grade, classroom structure, statement of the problem, and the teacher's goal.

2. Identify how the request for assistance was made. Was it made by a teacher or parent, or was it the result of an automatic referral process such as follow-up on an existing problem, excessive office referrals, etc.?

3. Provide any relevant background information.

4. Identify what has already been tried and the results.

5. Identify concerns, successes, and difficulties encountered.

6. Brainstorm additional strategies, resources, and ideas.

## Facilitating Training for Collaborative Problem-Solving Groups

Another way for an interventionist to create opportunities for reflection and professional growth is to facilitate the ongoing training of collaborative problem-solving groups. Teacher Assistance Teams, Multidisciplinary Teams, Prereferral Teams, or Care Teams might meet monthly to work on improving the quality of the services they provide to staff and students. The group might work on the efficiency of their meetings, as well as the effectiveness of their intervention plans. Each month the group might study one of the intervention booklets.

## Asking for Direct Feedback

The reflective interventionist may ask teachers, parents, and administrators with whom she has worked to give her feedback on the collaborative problem-solving process. What was helpful? How could the process be improved? By asking both general and specific questions, the interventionist gains insight to improve the process and her role in it.

## Conducting Staff Surveys

Surveys can yield valuable information for developing procedures to meet the needs of staff and students. To ensure a high rate of response, the interventionist can ask staff members to fill out a confidential survey during a staff meeting and to turn it in to a box as they leave the meeting. Figure 6-1 illustrates a sample staff survey.

# Chapter 6
## Skills of the Interventionist

### Figure 6-1

Dear Staff:

Please take a minute or two to respond to the survey below. Your responses will be anonymous. Your honest opinions will assist me as I continue to develop collaborative problem-solving relationships.

1. Have you received assistance with a student this year?  ☐ Yes  ☐ No

    If your answer to question 1 is "Yes," please continue with questions 3-10.
    If your answer to question 1 is "No," please complete question 2 only.

2. If "No," why not?
    - ☐ I did not have any severe problems with a student or students.
    - ☐ I did not know consultation services were available.
    - ☐ I prefer to handle things on my own.
    - ☐ I do not feel comfortable with _____, but did seek assistance from someone else in the school.

| (Please check the appropriate response.) | Not At All | Somewhat | Generally | Very Much So |
|---|---|---|---|---|
| 3. The interventionist was quick to respond to my concerns. | ☐ | ☐ | ☐ | ☐ |
| 4. The interventionist was sensitive to my concerns. | ☐ | ☐ | ☐ | ☐ |
| 5. The interventionist was easy to work with and listened to my ideas about how to solve the problem. | ☐ | ☐ | ☐ | ☐ |
| 6. Working with the interventionist was time efficient. | ☐ | ☐ | ☐ | ☐ |
| 7. The plan that was developed was organized and had clearly defined roles and timelines. | ☐ | ☐ | ☐ | ☐ |
| 8. The plan that was developed was practical (e.g., the amount of teacher time required was realistic). | ☐ | ☐ | ☐ | ☐ |
| 9. Adequate follow-up/support was provided after the plan was developed (e.g., modeling, coaching, etc.). | ☐ | ☐ | ☐ | ☐ |
| 10. The plan developed was effective (e.g., student behavior improved). | ☐ | ☐ | ☐ | ☐ |

NOTE: A copy of this form is provided in the "Reproducible Materials" at the end of this manual.

## Conclusion

No matter how skilled an interventionist is, there is always more to learn. By striving for professional growth each year—to improve communication and observation skills, to be more sensitive to the needs of staff members, and so on, the interventionist can become more proficient in both her technical knowledge and her ability to share that knowledge.

# CHAPTER 7

## Creating a Climate for Collaboration

ESTABLISHING A CLIMATE where staff members routinely engage in collaborative problem solving represents a fundamental shift in the way schools have traditionally functioned. Rather than operating in isolated classrooms, teachers seek assistance and provide support to one another. Rather than responding to problems when they have reached crisis proportions, staff members seek early resolution. However, this climate of cooperation is not created overnight. It develops with coordinated staff effort. The following procedures can assist in creating a climate for collaboration and remove roadblocks that may hamper such efforts.

## Developing Policies That Support Collaboration

The development of written discipline and responsibility policies facilitates the school-wide use of collaborative problem-solving strategies. In combination with the support and commitment of the building administrator, written policies can guarantee that at-risk students will receive collaborative services when needed. Key points in supporting school-wide collaboration include the following.

### Developing a School-Wide Mission Statement

A school-wide mission statement provides a staff with a common focus and an agreed upon purpose. Figure 7-1 shows a sample elementary school mission statement.

### Figure 7-1: Sample Mission Statement

We, the staff of Lincoln Elementary School, are committed to providing students with the behavioral and academic skills required to reason, communicate, and live with dignity in a literate society. Our staff members seek to provide instruction that allows all students to reach their fullest potential. We will assist students in gaining the academic competence and the responsibility required to find success through their school years and into the world of work.

Source: Reprinted with permission from Sprick, R., Sprick, M., & Garrison, M. (1992). *Foundations: Establishing positive discipline policies*. Longmont, CO: Sopris West.

When the statement reflects an "inclusive" philosophy—providing for all students—a foundation is laid to promote, encourage, and ultimately require staff to participate in collaborative intervention efforts to help at-risk students. Although most staff members intuitively strive to achieve the types of goals detailed in Figure 7-1, a written statement emphasizes and reinforces the school-wide commitment to an inclusive philosophy.

When staff members engage in collaborative practices, a few teachers may resist efforts to develop intervention plans. Without a mission statement, each teacher's personal philosophy is as valid as the next person's. However, when there is an agreed upon mission statement, the mission statement supersedes individual bias.

Teacher: *I've taught for twenty years. If students misbehave, it isn't tolerated. I send them out. It's not my problem.*

Administrator: *Our mission statement says that we will try to provide instruction that allows all students to reach their fullest potential. Sending them out of the room doesn't do that. I know that we are asking you to make changes, but I am willing to assist you in those changes. There are many things that we can do to help William learn to be responsible. We need to schedule some time to sit down and work out a plan for him. It may involve changes for you, but ultimately it will help William and the other students you work with learn to assume more responsibility for themselves, not less.*

Teacher: *After all this time teaching, I'm not about to start babying these kids along.*

Administrator: *Your experience has taught you many wonderful things about teaching. However, like all professionals—physicians, engineers, and so on—we need to continually expand our base of knowledge. Kids like William demand that we be well-informed. Throughout this year, we will be offering inservice opportunities to help all of us increase our skills. By helping kids like William, we are continually learning and improving the way we serve kids. There will be other Williams. Now, let's schedule a time when we can get together to establish a plan . . . .*

# Developing a Responsibility and Discipline Policy

An effective responsibility and discipline policy helps staff members work collaboratively to teach students how to be successful in the school setting. The policy should include clearly stated school-wide expectations as well as staff guidelines for teaching students how to meet the expectations. The guidelines should address the importance of working together to solve problems that are chronic or severe in nature. Figure 7-2 shows a sample of school-wide expectations and staff guidelines.

**Figure 7-2: Guidelines for Success and Staff Guidelines**

### Guidelines for Success

All staff and students at Lincoln Elementary School will work together to help everyone reach their fullest potential. Everyone will be treated with dignity and respect. Any behavior or action that helps someone grow and mature will be encouraged. Staff will keep students focused on our school guidelines, which follow:

1. Be responsible.
2. Always try.
3. Do your best.
4. Cooperate with others.
5. Treat everyone with dignity and respect.

Throughout the year, we will emphasize our school motto, "Be responsible. Do your best, and help the rest." These efforts will make Lincoln Elementary School a warm and exciting place where new learning occurs each and every day.

### Staff Guidelines for Teaching Student Responsibility and Discipline

All staff members contribute to Lincoln Elementary School's friendly, inviting environment. We set the tone through our actions and attitudes. Our continuous support and encouragement of students will be demonstrated through four important procedures.

1. We will teach students expectations for responsible behavior in every school environment by relating student actions to our guidelines for success. We will encourage students to be responsible, to always try, to do their best, to cooperate with others, and to treat everyone with dignity and respect.

2. We will provide positive feedback to students when they are meeting expectations and following the guidelines for success.

3. When minor misbehavior occurs, staff will view the misbehavior as a teaching opportunity, responding with calm, consistent corrections or consequences.

4. We will work collaboratively to solve problems that are chronic or severe in nature.

Source: Reprinted with permission from Sprick, R., Sprick, M., & Garrison, M. (1992). *Foundations: Establishing positive discipline policies*. Longmont, CO: Sopris West.

# Developing Written Descriptions of the Collaborative Services Available in the School

A written description of collaborative services should include information about all the services provided by various staff members and collaborative groups. For each service available, include:

- The purpose of the assistance.

- Clarification of the range of intervention services that may be offered.

    The roles of interventionist and the services provided tend to evolve over time as the needs of the staff change and the skills of the interventionist develop. Services may include: (1) discussing problems and successes with staff members; (2) conducting classroom observations; (3) completing diagnostic work; (4) arranging planning meetings between the teacher, the student, and the parents; (5) gathering relevant information about a student by reviewing records, talking to past teachers, or interviewing the parents; (6) assisting a teacher with the design of an intervention plan; (7) working directly with individuals or small groups of students to discuss problems, introduce plans, or conduct training; (8) assisting teachers with evaluation and revision of intervention plans; and (9) providing follow-up services and postintervention support.

- The amount of time available for the services provided.

    This information is important, and will vary widely depending upon the other responsibilities of the interventionist. For example, a school psychologist may only be able to devote one half day per week to intervention services due to the small amount of time spent in the building and other responsibilities.

- When the services are available.

    The interventionist should schedule time weekly specifically for intervention activities so that other tasks do not intrude. Some of this time should be allotted for observations and direct work with students, and some should be scheduled to permit before- or after-school meetings with teachers.

- How assistance can be requested.

    Procedures for initiating collaborative problem solving should be easy to access and clearly described. Procedures may involve completing a form or leaving a note for the interventionist.

Figure 7-3 shows a description of the collaborative services provided by a resource room teacher/consultant for special education students.

**Figure 7-3: Sample Job Description**

> The resource room teacher will provide two major services: (1) direct teaching to special education students based on each student's need for basic skill instruction as outlined in the student's individualized education plan (IEP); and (2) serving at least 20% of his time as a resource consultant—assisting classroom teachers with the design and implementation of interventions for special education students experiencing difficulty in regular classroom programs.
>
> In his capacity as interventionist, the resource room teacher can provide ideas and assistance for students experiencing both behavioral and academic difficulty. The types of help that may be provided include:
>
> - Lending an ear;
> - Helping to design intervention plans for the classroom;
> - Conducting observations;
> - Meeting directly with students and parents;
> - Designing motivational plans for students;
> - Participating as a mediator in teacher-student conferences;
> - Helping to adapt instructional practices for low performing students; and
> - Assisting with informal assessment. (Formal assessment for special education referral is conducted by the school psychologist.)
>
> There is no need to fill out a report or a form to start the ball rolling. Just leave a note in the resource teacher's box or schedule an appointment when you see him. Weekly student reports can be used to request additional time to discuss student progress.

Include the written descriptions in a staff handbook and/or distribute them to the staff. When intervention services are poorly defined or inadequately communicated, staff members are less likely to avail themselves of the services.

## Establishing Procedures for Automatic Referral of At-Risk Students

No matter how available collaborative problem-solving services might be, some teachers may not refer students. To ensure that needy students receive assistance, there should be a variety of ways to trigger intervention planning. Automatic referral systems set criteria for "red flagging" students who may need assistance. Criteria for automatic referral may include:

- A specified number of discipline referrals to the office, after-school detention, the time-out room, lunch time detention, or the homework room;
- A specified number of absences; or
- A specified minimum G.P.A. or a specified number of failing grades.

All automatic referral systems must be clearly described in the written responsibility and discipline policy. The description should include:

- How grades, office referrals, absenteeisms, etc. will be monitored;
- Who will be responsible for monitoring the grades, office referrals, absenteeism, etc.;

- Who will handle the referrals; and
- Who will decide what happens with the referral.

Automatic referral systems ensure that staff members work proactively to help students who are on a downward spiral. These systems are particularly important at the secondary level where teachers may not have the opportunity to notice the full magnitude of a student's problem.

## Developing an Organizational Diagram

Schematic diagrams or concept maps graphically depict the services that are available to help staff members implement their mission statement. Development of an organizational diagram (see Figure 7-4) often assists staff in utilizing a wide range of services.

**Figure 7-4: Sample Organizational Diagram**

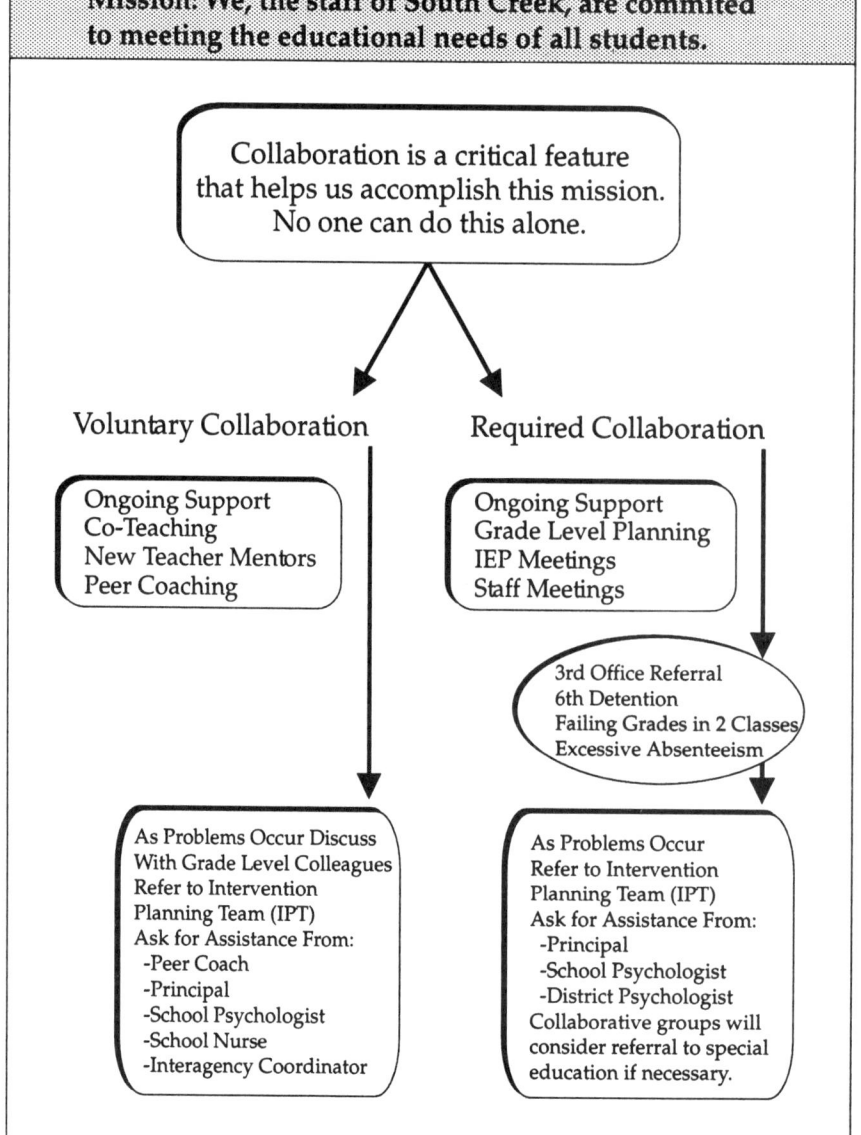

# Providing Ongoing Staff Development

An active staff development program creates an atmosphere of ongoing professional growth and collaboration. As staff members work together to develop new skills and strategies, it becomes clear that no one is expected to have all the answers. This basic message allays the misperception that all staff members should know how to reach every student and solve every problem. Seeking the professional opinions and assistance of colleagues becomes a natural part of the school's culture.

A strong mission statement helps focus staff development programs. Without an agreed upon mission, inservice often becomes a miscellaneous hodgepodge—with staff attending only those workshops that reinforce their own biases and interests. When staff development is guided by a mission statement, inservice activities are selected to help staff develop strategies that assist them in their efforts to implement the mission statement.

# Removing Roadblocks to School-Wide Collaboration

In many schools, collaboration must be facilitated by identifying and removing roadblocks. Major roadblocks to collaboration often include concerns regarding confidentiality, a fear that the process may affect teacher evaluations, and a concern that collaboration will require much time. Once roadblocks are removed, initially reticent staff may begin cautiously experimenting with some form of collaborative problem solving.

## Protecting the Confidentiality of Those Served

Those who serve on collaborative planning teams and/or as interventionists must make a commitment to protect the confidentiality of the students, teachers, and parents they discuss and assist. Staff should be informed that confidentiality will be maintained, and those involved in collaborative planning must honor this commitment.

## Clearly Defining How Collaborative Efforts Are Related to Staff Evaluation

Some staff members may hesitate to engage in collaborative problem solving if they think it will be related negatively to staff evaluation. To reduce this problem, staff members and the administration should jointly determine in advance how available collaborative structures might be related to teacher evaluation. Figure 7-5 shows such relationships in a hypothetical school.

### Figure 7-5: Sample Correlations of Collaborative Services and Staff Evaluation

| Collaborative Services Available | Reports On Collaborative Relationship Given to Admin.? | Relationship to Staff Evaluation |
|---|---|---|
| Peer Coaches | No | None |
| Co-Teaching | No | None |
| Consultation With Special Ed. Staff | Only as related to placement decisions for identified special education students. | None |
| Mentors for New Staff | Mentor provides progress reports to administrator twice during probationary year. | Admin. may use info. from mentor as part of evaluation. |
| District Behavior Specialist | Yes | None |
| School Counselor | No | None |
| School Psychologist | Only as related to placement decisions for identified special education students. | None |
| School Nurse | No—unless a student has a health issue that must be reported. | None |
| Lead Teacher | No | None |
| Grade Level Staffings | No | None |
| Intervention Planning Team (IPT) Meetings | Administrator may take part in the meeting. | None |
| Multidisciplinary Team Meetings (MDT)/IEP Meetings | Administrator may take part in the meeting. | None |
| Administrative Coaching | Observations and consultation conducted directly by administrative staff. | None—unless related to identified goal for that staff person. |
| Formal Teacher Evaluation | Administrator conducts the evaluation. | These observations and conferences make up the sum total of formal evaluation unless the staff member has been otherwise notified. |

# Creating Time for Collaboration

Lack of time is the greatest roadblock to collaboration. Unfortunately, it is also the most difficult obstacle to overcome. Resources available for intervention planning vary tremendously from state to state, district to district, and building to building (see Figure 7-6.) Each staff must determine its own priorities, evaluate the resources it has available, and then work to create the time that is needed.

Figure 7-6: Variability in Resources

| Elementary School A | Elementary School B |
|---|---|
| 800 students | 350 students |
| Average class size—35 | Average class size—25 |
| 1 administrator | 1 administrator |
| Half-time counselor | Full-time counselor |
| Half-time school psychologist | Half-time school psychologist |
| Librarian<br>Music specialist | Librarian<br>Music specialist<br>P.E. specialist<br>Computer teacher |
| | Lead teacher (available half-time for collaboration) |
| | District-level behavior specialist (on call) |

In many schools, staff members are stretched to the limit. For example, School A, described in Figure 7-6, will obviously have a very difficult time finding the time and staff resources necessary to assist with intervention planning. School B, on the other hand, has fewer students with more staff time allocated. There is more time available with the counselor. There is also a lead teacher who can assist with intervention planning, and the school has access to a district-level specialist. In addition to the services of these people, the general education staff has more discretionary time for intervention planning because their students are taught by specialists in music, P.E., and so on. Even in schools such as School A, however, limited resources can sometimes be used more effectively if collaborative problem solving is a priority. Suggestions include:

- Identifying staff who might be available to cover classes.

  In most schools, some staff time can be allocated for covering the classes of teachers involved in collaborative intervention planning. When possible, staff members and the times they have available should be identified ahead of time (see Figure 7-7). Then when an interventionist responds to requests for assistance, this information can be used to arrange meeting times with teachers.

**Figure 7-7: Master Schedule of Resources for Covering Classes**

### Schedule for Covering Classes—By Appointment Only!

**For the week of** _Feb. 5-9_

Don't forget to leave a note in our box if you need one of us to cover a class. Also be sure to identify the room and the activity.

Mr. Gilroy (Counselor)

Wednesday, _Feb. 7_

- 1:30-1:45   Marjorie Johnson, Rm. 10—show film/intervention planning w/ Mrs. Y.
- 1:45-:2:00  Marjorie Johnson, Rm. 10—show film/intervention planning w/ Mrs. Y.
- 2:00-2:15
- 2:15-2:30

Mrs. Yoshida (Asst. Principal)

Wednesday, _Feb. 7_

- 9:00-9:15
- 9:15-9:30

Friday, _Feb. 9_

- 10:00-10:15   Not available—Sorry, district meeting/see alternative times.
- 10:15-10:30   Not available—Sorry, district meeting/see alternative times.
- 10:30-10:45

Ms. Torgeson (Teacher Asst.)

Monday, _Feb. 5_

- 9:00-9:15
- 9:15-9:30
- 9:30-9:45
- 9:45-10:00
- 2:00-2:15
- 2:15-2:30

Tuesday, _Feb. 6_

- 9:00-9:15
- 9:15-9:30
- 9:30-9:45
- 9:45-10:00

# Chapter 7
## Creating a Climate for Collaboration

A notebook of appointment times could be kept in the office. Whenever a time is scheduled, a note would be given to the staff member who will cover the class.

- Setting up times when teachers cover for each other.

Collaborative problem solving can occur in a variety of ways—through peer coaching activities, teacher mentor programs, grade level groups, with an interventionist, or within Teacher Assistance Teams (or similar team formats). These activities can be assisted by having pairs of teachers cover for each other. For example, third and fifth grade teachers might agree to take turns covering each other's classes every other week. The teachers could plan mixed age level activities for the students and be free to collaborate with grade level colleagues every other week.

- Providing weekly or monthly collaboration time.

Recognizing the importance of collegial planning time, some districts regularly schedule early releases or late starts. These schedules allow for longer planning periods, but do not reduce student contact time. For example, students who normally leave school each day at 2:30 P.M. would stay until 2:45 P.M. four days per week, and go home at 1:30 P.M. one day each week. This allows concentrated planning time, and being able to manipulate the schedule gives the staff greater flexibility.

Figure 7-8 illustrates how early release time might be used effectively. In Schedule 1, there is a 20 minute general staff meeting, followed by 30 minutes of intervention planning time (from 2:00 P.M. to 2:30 P.M.). Depending on the staff size and the demand for services, one or more planning groups could operate at the same time. Staff members who are not involved in intervention planning are free to work in their rooms from 2:00 P.M. until 4:00 P.M. Those participating in intervention planning have from 2:30 P.M. to 4:00 P.M. for their discretionary work time.

**Figure 7-8**

| Schedule 1 | Schedule 2 |
|---|---|
| Staff Meeting 1:30 -1:50 | Grade Level Planning—1:35-3:30 |
| Work Time 1:50-4:00 | Intervention Planning 3:00-3:30 |
| Intervention Planning 2:00-2:30 | Work Time 3:30-4:00 |

In Schedule 2, grade level teams meet for one hour and 55 minutes. One hour and 25 minutes is spent collaboratively planning instruction, while the last 30 minutes is spent on intervention planning. This leaves 30 minutes of discretionary time to be used for either individual work time or continued planning, if desired.

While this type of flexible scheduling provides many options for intervention planning that traditional schedules do not, it requires masterful bus scheduling, communication, and careful consideration of childcare options in the neighborhood. Parental support can be fostered where there is a clear understanding that staff time can be used more effectively to plan for students and that student contact time will not be reduced. Through clear communication with parents, and opportunities to discuss the pros and cons in advance, communities will often support these scheduling options.

Lack of time and resources will always be significant impediments to collaboration. However, with perseverance and creativity, most obstacles can be overcome.

# Inviting Staff to Use Collaborative Services

Sometimes staff members need to be both educated and sold on the benefits of collaboration. Interventionists must be invitational, and they may also have to actively "market" themselves if they hope to encourage the voluntary use of their services. Possible marketing suggestions include:

## Mini Presentations

At various points throughout the year, interventionists and collaborative teams can give brief (one-two minute) presentations to remind staff members of their services. The presentations may involve a quick role play or skit; they may be funny or straightforward—but they should be informative.

## Posters and Fliers

Figure 7-9 shows a sample "ad" for the services of a interventionist. It uses a humorous format to provide staff members with specific information about ways to make a referral. Ads can be posted in the faculty room, run off on brightly colored paper and put in staff mailboxes, or distributed at faculty meetings.

**Figure 7-9**

---

**Notice: Job Wanted!**

**School Psychologist** at Filmore Elementary is looking for work as a consultant and helper to classroom teachers. Skills include discipline ideas, student motivation techniques, and strategies for students struggling academically. Two heads are sometimes better than one, so use my head and together we can develop ideas for helping those at-risk students in your classroom. Act now! I might be able to help before the situation has gone on so long that you are considering special education referral. No paperwork is required! (Yea!) Just let me know and we can set up a time to talk. Please note, I don't feel like I have ANSWERS, per se, but by working together we can probably come up with some pretty good plans.

---

## Testimonials

Contemporary print and video advertising demonstrate the power of the testimonial. Having someone extol the benefits of a product or service is one of the most effective ways of convincing others of its value. Distributing a short report on a successful intervention by a teacher who has worked with the interventionist or a problem-solving team will both market the collaborative service and disseminate a successful practice.

## Memos

A memo is another simple but effective means of reminding staff members that there are services available. Figure 7-10 shows a sample memo that could be placed in the mailboxes of middle school teachers in the early spring.

**Figure 7-10**

---

**Memo**

Date:  March 1

To:  All Staff

Re:  Collaborative Intervention Planning

*Spring is here . . .*

*The flowers bloom.*

*The birds return.*

***The adolescents turn weird!***

Last year about this time, we started having a significant increase in the number of severe discipline incidents. Don't forget about us. We'd love to help you with those challenging behavioral and motivational problems. Just drop one of us a note and we can meet to knock around ideas.

Sincerely,
Ms. Almquist, Vice Principal
Mr. Welsh, Resource Teacher
Miss Saito, Counselor
Ms. Young, School Psychologist
The Grade Level Assistance Teams
The School-Wide Assistance Team

---

## Conclusion

The school environment can be structured to facilitate collaborative planning for at-risk students. This can be accomplished by creatively assisting teachers in finding the time to collaborate and removing other roadblocks such as confidentiality. Policies that support collaboration and ongoing staff development communicate that working together is a highly professional endeavor and an effective way to help students who are most at-risk of failure in school and eventually in the community.

# References

Bauer, A.M. & Sapona, R.H. (1991). *Managing classrooms to facilitate learning.* Englewood Cliffs, NJ: Prentice Hall.

Cangelosi, J.S. (1988). *Classroom management strategies: Gaining and maintaining students' cooperation.* Whiteplains, NY: Longman.

Carr, E.G. & Durand, V.M. (1986). The social-communicative basis of severe behavior problems in children. In S. Reiss & R. Bootzin (Eds.), *Theoretical issues in behavior therapy.* New York: Academic Press.

Charles, C.M. (1989). *Building classroom discipline: From models to practice* (3rd ed.). Whiteplains, NY: Longman.

Colvin, G. (1992). *Managing acting-out behavior: A staff development program.* Eugene, OR: Behavior Associates. (Distributed by Sopris West, Longmont, CO.)

Colvin, G. & Sugai, G. (1989). *Managing escalating behavior* (2nd ed.). Eugene, OR: Behavior Associates.

Cullinan, D. & Epstein, M.H. (1985). Behavioral interventions for educating adolescents with behavior disorders. *The Pointer, 30*(1), 4-7.

Cunningham, R.C. & Shillington, N.M. (1990). Mentoring preservice teachers through interdisciplinary teams: A school university partnership. *Action in Teacher Education, 11*(4), 6-12.

Emmer, E.T., Evertson, C.M., Sanford, J.P., Clements, B.S., & Worsham, M.E. (1984). *Classroom management for secondary teachers.* Englewood Cliffs, NJ: Prentice Hall.

Evertson, C.M., Emmer, E.T., Clements, B.S., Sanford, J.P., & Worsham, M.E. (1984). *Classroom management for elementary teachers.* Englewood Cliffs, NJ: Prentice Hall.

Great Falls Public Schools. (1993). *Responding to individual differences in education* (7th ed.). Longmont, CO: Sopris West.

Kerr, M.M. & Nelson, C.M. (1989). *Strategies for managing behavior problems in the classroom* (2nd ed.). NY: Macmillan.

Lavigna, G.L. & Donnellan, A.M. (1986). *Alternatives to punishment: Solving behavior problems with nonaversive strategies.* New York: Irvington.

Lovitt, T.C. (1991). *Preventing school dropouts: Tactics for at-risk, remedial, and mildly handicapped adolescents.* Austin, TX: Pro-Ed.

Morgan, D.P. & Jenson, W.R. (1988). *Teaching behaviorally disordered students: Preferred practices.* Columbus, OH: Merrill Publishing.

Nelson, C.M. & Rutherford, R.B., Jr. (1988). Behavioral interventions with behaviorally disordered students. In M.C. Wang, M.C. Reynolds, & H.J. Walberg (Eds.), *Handbook of special education: Research and practice* (vol. 2, pp. 125-153). Oxford, England: Pergamon Press.

Phillips, V. & McCullough, L. (1992). *Student/Staff support teams.* Longmont, CO: Sopris West.

Rhode, G., Jenson, W.R., & Reavis, H.K. (1992). *The tough kid book: Practical classroom management strategies.* Longmont, CO: Sopris West.

Sprick, R.S. (1981). *The solution book: A guide to classroom discipline.* Chicago: Science Research Associates.

Sprick, R.S. (1985). *Discipline in the secondary classroom: A problem by problem survival guide.* West Nyack, NY: Center for Applied Research in Education.

Sprick, R., Sprick, M., & Garrison, M. (1992). *Foundations: Establishing positive discipline policies* (Vol. II). Longmont, CO: Sopris West.

Sugai, G.M. & Tindal, G.A. (1993). *Effective school consultation: An interactive approach* (p. 34). Pacific Grove, CA: Brooks/Cole Publishing.

Sulzer-Azaroff, B. & Mayer, G.R. (1987). *Achieving educational excellence: Using behavioral strategies.* New York: Holl, Rinehart, and Winston.

Van de Werfhost, F.H. (1986). Temperament and teacher-child interactions. In G.A. Kohnstamm (Ed.), *Temperament discussed: Temperament and development in infancy and childhood* (pp. 141-147). Leiden, the Netherlands: University of Leiden.

VanGundy, A.B. (1987). *Creative problem solving: A guide for trainers and management.* New York: Quorum Books.

VanHouten, R., Axelrod, S., Bailey, J.S., Favell, J.E., Foxx, R.M., Iwata, B.A., & Lovaas, O.I. (1988). The right to effective behavioral treatment. *Journal of Applied Behavior Analysis, 21,* 381-384.

Walker, H.M. & Severson, H.H. (1992). *Systematic screening for behavior disorders* (2nd ed.). Longmont, CO: Sopris West.

# Reproducible Materials

*T*he following form(s) may assist you in implementing the *Interventions* program.

These pages may be reproduced without permission from the publisher.

# Informal Request for Assistance

Date:
To:
From:                    Position:
Re.:

**Brief description of the problem:**




☐ This is an informal request for assistance.
   (I'd just like some ideas at this point.)

☐ This is a request for formal assistance.
   (The problem may be serious enough for a structured intervention plan.)

---

# Informal Request for Assistance

Date:
To:
From:                    Position:
Re.:

**Brief description of the problem:**




☐ This is an informal request for assistance.
   (I'd just like some ideas at this point.)

☐ This is a request for formal assistance.
   (The problem may be serious enough for a structured intervention plan.)

*Interventions: Collaborative Planning for Students at Risk* • Copyright © 1993 by Sprick, Sprick, & Garrison

# Formal Request for Assistance

| | |
|---|---|
| Referring Person | |
| Position | Date |
| Student | |
| Grade | DOB / / Sex: ☐ M ☐ F IEP: ☐ Y ☐ N |

## Check the Type of Problem Behavior

**Academic:** ☐ Reading ☐ Spelling ☐ Writing ☐ Study Skills
☐ Other_____

**Social:** ☐ Aggression ☐ Noncompliance ☐ Truancy ☐ Tardies
☐ Withdrawal ☐ Disruptions ☐ Social Skills ☐ Self-Management
☐ Other_____

**Communication:** ☐ Language ☐ Fluency ☐ Articulation ☐ Voice
☐ Other_____

**Self-Help:** ☐ Dressing ☐ Hygiene ☐ Other_____

**Health:** ☐ Vision ☐ Hearing ☐ Physical ☐ Other_____

## Provide a Specific and Observable Description of the Problem



## Provide a Specific Description of the Problem Context

Where:

When:

With Whom:

Other:

## Provide a List of Previous Remediation Attempts (If Any)

1.
2.
3.

Source: Adapted with permission from Sugai, G.M. & Tindal, G.A. (1993). *Effective school consultation: An integrative approach.* Pacific Grove, CA: Brooks/Cole Publishing.

*Interventions: Collaborative Planning for Students at Risk* • Copyright © 1993 by Sprick, Sprick, & Garrison

# Parental Permission Form for Intervention

Dear _____:

The staff of _____ strive to help all children feel a part of our learning community. Occasionally, we find that one of our students can benefit from additional assistance. We would like to provide _____ with special support.

The goal of this assistance will be to help your child learn to:

_____

Assistance may include, but is not limited to: reviews of the student's school file; informal academic assessment—reviewing work samples and habits, conducting an informal reading inventory; asking teachers about work habits and classroom behavior; classroom observations by a specialist; and the development of a supportive intervention plan developed by teachers and specialists in our building.

We need your permission to proceed with this assistance. Please sign the attached form and return it to _____ by _____.

If you have any questions, feel free to call _____ at _____ between the hours of _____.

We look forward to working with you and your child.

Sincerely,

- - - - - - - - - - - - - - - - - - - - - - - - - - - - - - - - - - - - - - - - - - - - - -

### Parental Authorization for Student Assistance

Please check the appropriate box.

☐ Permission is granted to provide student assistance as described above.
☐ Permission is denied because _____

_____

_____

_____     _____
(Parent/Guardian Signature)         (Date)

*Interventions: Collaborative Planning for Students at Risk* • Copyright © 1993 by Sprick, Sprick, & Garrison

# Observation Form

| Student(s) | Teacher |
|---|---|
| Date | Time |
| Subject/Activity | |

| Time | Description of Student Behavior | Description of Teacher Interaction |
|---|---|---|
|  |  |  |

*Interventions: Collaborative Planning for Students at Risk* • Copyright © 1993 by Sprick, Sprick, & Garrison

# 25 Minute Intervention Planning Process

Student Name _____ Age _____ Grade _____ Date _____
Interventionist Name _____ Teacher(s) Name(s) _____
_____
Other Participants _____

Starting Time _____

## Step 1: Background (6 Minutes)   Stop _____

- Describe the presenting problem. Identify when, where, how often, how long, etc. the problem occurs.



- Identify student strengths.



- Identify strategies already tried.



## Step 2: Problem and Goal (2 Minutes)   Stop _____

- Narrow the scope of the problem and identify a goal.



## Step 3: Responsible and Irresponsible Behavior (4 Minutes)   Stop _____

- Provide examples of responsible behavior and/or student strengths to encourage.
- Provide examples of irresponsible behavior to discourage.

| **Responsible Behavior** | **Irresponsible Behavior** |
| --- | --- |
|  |  |

*Interventions: Collaborative Planning for Students at Risk* • Copyright © 1993 by Sprick, Sprick, & Garrison

## Step 4: Consequences (2 Minutes)    Stop _____

- Determine whether irresponsible or inappropriate behavior will be corrected, ignored, or whether a consequence will be implemented.

## Step 5: Proactive Strategies (4 Minutes)    Stop _____

- Brainstorm strategies to encourage responsible behavior. (Brainstorm, don't evaluate.)

## Step 6: Proactive Plan (3 Minutes)    Stop _____

- Select a manageable set of proactive strategies to implement.

## Step 7: Final Details (4 Minutes)    Stop _____

**a. Evaluation:**

- Identify at least two ways to determine if the plan is working.

**b. Support:**

- Identify things other adults can do to assist the student and teacher. (Be specific—who, what, where, when.)

**c. Plan Summary:**

- Identify each person's responsibilities and when actions will be taken;
- Identify who will discuss the plan with the student and when; and
- Schedule follow-up.

| Who | Responsibilities | Date(s) |
|-----|------------------|---------|
|     |                  |         |
|     |                  |         |
|     |                  |         |

Discussion With the Student:
Who _____ Date _____ Time _____

Follow-Up Meeting:
Who _____ Date _____ Time _____

*Interventions: Collaborative Planning for Students at Risk* • Copyright © 1993 by Sprick, Sprick, & Garrison

# Intervention Summary Form

Student _____ Date _____

Teacher(s) _____

Other Participants _____

**Goal:**

**Student Responsibilities:**

**Teacher Responsibilities:**

**Interventionist Responsibilities:**

**Parent/Guardian Responsibilities:**

**Follow-Up:**

*Interventions: Collaborative Planning for Students at Risk* • Copyright © 1993 by Sprick, Sprick, & Garrison

# Intervention Decision Guide (IDG)

Student Name _____ Age _____ Grade _____ Beginning Date _____
Interventionist Name _____ Teacher(s) Name(s) _____

Other Participants _____

## Stage 1: Background

**R**eason for the Referral and Description of the Problem(s)




**C**ode Red (Is it an emergency situation?)

The behavior is a threat to physical safety.

If true, implement Intervention A:
*Managing Physically Dangerous Behavior.*

The behavior is so disruptive the teacher can't teach.

If true, implement Intervention B:
*Managing Severely Disruptive Behavior.*

**Notes:**



**N**otes on the Problem(s)   What, Where, When, Why

Are there situations that seem to set off the problem behavior?


Where do the problem(s) tend to occur?


When do the problem(s) tend to occur?
   Time(s) of day:
   Day(s) of the week:
Are there situations in which the problem(s) seem less prevalent?

How often do the problem(s) occur? How long does the behavior last?

What seems to be maintaining (reinforcing) the student's misbehavior? (Check as many as apply.)

☐ Attention        ☐ Venting frustration or anger        ☐ Other _____
☐ Power            ☐ Escape                              _____

**Notes:**

1.

*Interventions: Collaborative Planning for Students at Risk* • Copyright © 1993 by Sprick, Sprick, & Garrison

## Strengths of the Student (at Least Three)

## The Teacher(s)' Goal or Desired Outcome
What would the teacher(s) like to have happen? What can't the teacher(s) "live with" any longer?

## Notes on Parental Involvement
Contact date(s):
Notes on the contact(s):

What would the parent(s) or guardian like to have happen?

## Input From the Student

## Other Information
Input from previous teachers:

Input from other staff who know the student (assistants, counselor, specialists, etc.):

Review of the student's records:

## Interventions Tried and Their Results
Description:

How long attempted?
How successful?

# Stage 2: Preparation

## Goal or Desired Outcome for the Intervention

## Possible Interventions to Consider

| Descriptor | Intervention | Check the intervention(s) to consider. | Check the intervention(s) selected. |
|---|---|---|---|
| (If the statement is true, consider including this intervention as part of the plan.) | | | |
| The behavior poses a threat to someone's physical safety. | **Intervention A:** *Managing Physically Dangerous Behavior* | | |
| The behavior is so severe that the teacher cannot continue to teach. | **Intervention B:** *Managing Severely Disruptive Behavior* | | |
| The student may not know what is expected. | **Intervention C:** *Planned Discussions* | | |
| The student may have an underlying academic problem. | **Intervention D:** *Academic Assistance* | | |
| The student makes negative comments about himself/herself and/or others. | **Intervention E:** *Restructuring Self-Talk* | | |
| The student seems to be unaware of when he/she engages in inappropriate behavior. | **Intervention F:** *Signal Interference Cueing* | | |
| The student would benefit from additional adult support and attention. | **Intervention G:** *Mentoring* | | |
| The student is impulsive and has difficulty maintaining emotional control. | **Intervention H:** *Self-Control Training* | | |
| The student has difficulty with motivation and may not understand how to reach a goal. | **Intervention I:** *Goal Setting and Contracting* | | |
| The student does not know how to meet expectations. | **Intervention J:** *Teaching Desired Behaviors* | | |
| The student has some motivation to change or learn new behaviors. | **Intervention K:** *Self-Monitoring* | | |
| The misbehavior is a *firmly* established part of the student's behavior. | **Intervention L:** *Structured Reinforcement Systems* | | |
| The teacher(s) feel anxious, worried, discouraged, or angry about a student or students. | **Intervention M:** *Managing Stress* | | |
| Several students in a class have difficulty managing their behavior. | **Intervention N:** *Classroom Management Strategies* | | |
| The student gets a lot of attention from adults and/or peers for misbehavior or failure. | **Intervention O:** *Increasing Positive Interactions* | | |
| It is difficult to be consistent with the student because it is not always clear when the student has crossed the line between appropriate and inappropriate behavior. and/or Consequences for misbehavior seem necessary, but do not seem to work. | **Intervention P:** *Borderlines and Consequences* | | |

# Stage 3: Intervention Design

## Selected Intervention(s)

## Summary of Responsibilities for Implementing the Plan
Specify who is responsible for doing what. Establish timelines for implementation.

## Methods for Evaluating Intervention Effectiveness
Specify at least two sources of evaluation information.

## Summary of Final Plan
Interventionist: On the "Intervention Summary Sheet," summarize and distribute a final copy of responsibilities.

# Stage 4: Implementation

## Initial Follow-Up Notes

## Follow-Up #1
Date of the follow-up meeting:
Purpose of the follow-up meeting:
Summary of the follow-up meeting:

## Follow-Up #2
Date of the follow-up meeting:
Purpose of the follow-up meeting:
Summary of the follow-up meeting:

# Intervention Summary Sheet

Date

Student(s)          Age        Grade

Teacher(s)

Other Participants

**Goal(s)**

| Date | Action(s) | Responsibility |
|------|-----------|----------------|
|      |           |                |

*Interventions: Collaborative Planning for Students at Risk* • Copyright © 1993 by Sprick, Sprick, & Garrison

# Staff Survey

Dear Staff:

Please take a minute or two to respond to the survey below. Your responses will be anonymous. Your honest opinions will assist me as I continue to develop collaborative problem-solving relationships.

1. Have you received assistance with a student this year?  ☐ Yes  ☐ No

    If your answer to question 1 is "Yes," please continue with questions 3-10.
    If your answer to question 1 is "No," please complete question 2 only.

2. If "No," why not?
    - ☐ I did not have any severe problems with a student or students.
    - ☐ I did not know consultation services were available.
    - ☐ I prefer to handle things on my own.
    - ☐ I do not feel comfortable with _____, but did seek assistance from someone else in the school.

| (Please check the appropriate response.) | Not At All | Somewhat | Generally | Very Much So |
|---|---|---|---|---|
| 3. The interventionist was quick to respond to my concerns. | ☐ | ☐ | ☐ | ☐ |
| 4. The interventionist was sensitive to my concerns. | ☐ | ☐ | ☐ | ☐ |
| 5. The interventionist was easy to work with and listened to my ideas about how to solve the problem. | ☐ | ☐ | ☐ | ☐ |
| 6. Working with the interventionist was time efficient. | ☐ | ☐ | ☐ | ☐ |
| 7. The plan that was developed was organized and had clearly defined roles and timelines. | ☐ | ☐ | ☐ | ☐ |
| 8. The plan that was developed was practical (e.g., the amount of teacher time required was realistic). | ☐ | ☐ | ☐ | ☐ |
| 9. Adequate follow-up/support was provided after the plan was developed (e.g., modeling, coaching, etc.). | ☐ | ☐ | ☐ | ☐ |
| 10. The plan developed was effective (e.g., student behavior improved). | ☐ | ☐ | ☐ | ☐ |

# ORDER FORM

*To* ORDER additional copies of *Interventions: Collaborative Planning for Students At Risk* please mail or FAX this order form or phone toll free with credit card orders. Purchase orders are also accepted (via FAX or mail).

| CODE # | DESCRIPTION | PRICE | QTY. | COST |
|---|---|---|---|---|
| 49MAN | Interventions: Collaborative Planning for Students At Risk (Procedural Manual and 16 Intervention Booklets) | $65.00 | | |
| 49TAPE | Interventions Audio Tape Album | $59.00 | | |
| 49MT | **Buy both and save.** Interventions Procedural Manual, 16 Intervention Booklets, and Audio Tape Album | $112.50 | | |
| Intervention Booklets are also available in packets of 10 each: | | | | |
| 49PAKA | Intervention A: *Managing Physically Dangerous Behavior* | $18.00 | | |
| 49PAKB | Intervention B: *Managing Severely Disruptive Behavior* | $18.00 | | |
| 49PAKC | Intervention C: *Planned Discussions* | $18.00 | | |
| 49PAKD | Intervention D: *Academic Assistance* | $40.00 | | |
| 49PAKE | Intervention E: *Restructuring Self-Talk* | $18.00 | | |
| 49PAKF | Intervention F: *Signal Interference Cueing* | $18.00 | | |
| 49PAKG | Intervention G: *Mentoring* | $18.00 | | |
| 49PAKH | Intervention H: *Self-Control Training* | $25.00 | | |
| 49PAKI | Intervention I: *Goal Setting and Contracting* | $25.00 | | |
| 49PAKJ | Intervention J: *Teaching Desired Behaviors* | $18.00 | | |
| 49PAKK | Intervention K: *Self-Monitoring* | $18.00 | | |
| 49PAKL | Intervention L: *Structured Reinforcement Systems* | $25.00 | | |
| 49PAKM | Intervention M: *Managing Stress* | $18.00 | | |
| 49PAKN | Intervention N: *Classroom Management Strategies* | $25.00 | | |
| 49PAKO | Intervention O: *Increasing Positive Interactions* | $25.00 | | |
| 49PAKP | Intervention P: *Borderlines and Consequences* | $25.00 | | |
| — | Sopris West Catalog of Programs | FREE | | |
| ** 10% of cost, $3.00 minimum. | | Shipping/Handling** | | |
| | | TOTAL COST OF THIS ORDER | | |

**Billing Address**

_____
_____
_____
_____

Phone _____

**Shipping Address**   Same as billing address? ☐

_____
_____
_____
_____

Phone _____

**Method of Payment**

○ VISA  ○ MasterCard  ○ Check/Money Order  ○ Purchase Order No. _____
*(Make payable to: Sopris West.)*   *(Copy of P.O. MUST be enclosed.)*

| | | | | | | | | | | | | | | |  Credit Card Expiration Date | | | / | | |
*(Credit Card Number)*   MONTH   YEAR

_____   _____
*(Please print name of cardholder.)*   *(Cardholder please sign here.)*

## 3 EASY WAYS TO ORDER

**1** — **Call Toll Free:** 1-800-547-6747

**2** — **Mail Order Form:** Sopris West, 1140 Boston Avenue, P.O. Box 1809, Longmont, CO 80502-1809

**3** — **FAX:** 1-303-776-5934

# Give Us Feedback

Your Name: _____
Title or Position: _____
Address: _____
_____

Interventions that are not included in the 1993 edition of *Interventions*, that should be included in the next edition:
_____
_____
_____

A model plan that I used for _____ that is not included in
                              (please specify the *Intervention* title)
the 1993 edition of *Interventions* was:
(Attach additional sheets if necessary.)
_____
_____
_____
_____
_____
_____

If the plan you described above is used in the revision, please specify if you would like your name included in the booklet.

❑ Yes, please include my name if the plan above is used in the revision.

Authorization signature required _____

❑ No, include the suggested plan above, but do not use my name.

**Return completed form to:**
Randall Sprick c/o
Editor • Sopris West • 1140 Boston Avenue • Longmont, CO 80501